A
BORDER
TOO
HIGH

A GUIDE
TO
WARTIME CRASHES
IN THE
BORDER HILLS

PETER CLARK

A
BORDER
TOO HIGH

A GUIDE TO WARTIME CRASHES
IN THE BORDER HILLS

Peter Clark

©Peter Clark, 1999

ISBN 1 900038 30 7

Published by
GLEN GRAPHICS
4 Ryecroft Park, Wooler, Northumberland NE71 6AS
Tel/Fax: 01668 281249
E-mail: info@glengraphics.co.uk
Web site: www.glengraphics.co.uk

Contents

LOCATION MAP

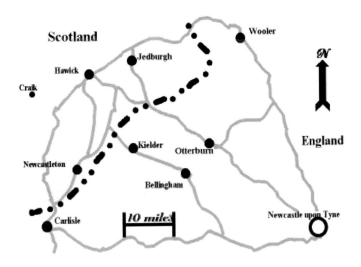

Acknowledgements

The contents of this book are a mixture of the memories of people of the Border area, surviving wartime aircrew and facts recorded in official documents at the time the events took place. Although everyone's contribution was important there are several people without whose knowledge it would have been impossible to even consider making a start on the project.

First among these is Robert Anderson whose almost encyclopaedic knowledge of the people and geography of Upper Redesdale and the North Tyne Valley provided me with many contacts in that area. In particular he introduced me to David "Mac" Rogerson who was able to refer to his father's diaries regarding the events of nearly 60 years ago. Similarly, Charlie Armstrong was able to provide me with information about people and places in the extreme western area of the region. I am indebted to both of these two men for without their initial help the local knowledge element of the stories would not have come to light.

The area north of the Border provided me with a greater challenge as even my farming connections do not extend there. But eventually after several false starts I found Jack and Mary Patterson of Newcastleton who not only provided me with information but also put me in contact with other people having memories of the period. I am extremely grateful to them for that help and also for their forbearance and hospitality on a day when the Border weather was a little short on the latter commodity.

The memories of surviving aircrew are perhaps the best source of information about any crash and I am extremely grateful to George Dove CGM; DFM and Mark Niman DFM for patiently providing details of their respective experiences. This would not have been possible had Frank Linin not put me in touch with George Dove. Frank Linin was an evacuee at Slaggyford during the war and as a young boy the crash of a Whitley bomber there in 1940 made a particular impression him. In recent years he has researched the crash of this aircraft and its crew in great detail and as a result of this eventually located George Dove. I am extremely grateful that he felt able to share this knowledge with me.

Once again Flt. Lt. Maggie Pleasant, the Community Relations Officer at RAF Leeming has found material in the station archive for me and also provided photographs of recent visits by surviving aircrew. Maggie is a very busy lady and I greatly appreciated her making time to accommodate my enquiries.

The staff at all the archive centres from which I have obtained information have always been courteous and efficient. They deserve thanks for their patience in fielding questions about the whereabouts of documents and also for their suggestions as to the possibilities of other avenues of inquiry. These organisations include the Public Record Officer, Kew, the Royal Air Force Museum Hendon (Department of Research and Information Services), the Air Historical Branch of the Ministry of Defence, the Northumberland County Record Office, Morpeth and the Scottish Borders Archive and Local History Centre, Selkirk.

I am also indebted to the Commonwealth War Graves Commission and the Volksbund Deutsche Kreigsgraberfürsorge for providing details regarding the unfortunate casualties.

Thanks to Mike Allport and Alan Gilholm from the publishers whose advice and expertise have once again helped get an idea into printed form.

Lastly I must also thank my friends and family not only for their encouragement but also for their tolerance of what can sometimes become an overpowering and all consuming interest. In this regard my wife, Chris, must have special mention for she it is who puts up with the scraps of paper left by the phone, the lack of attention to household duties when the opportunity of a good walking day to the hills beckons and all the other doubtless annoying traits which seem to be part of the baggage of unfulfilled inquisitiveness. But at least I am now out of her kitchen!

Introduction

Apart from short stretches at both its western and eastern extremities the Border between England and Scotland lies across high ground. Much of this area is of a wild, desolate, and isolated moorland nature. Such peaks that do thrust skyward from this rolling upland are gently round topped hills rather than the classic, archetypal, rocky summits of the Lake District or Snowdonia. These peaks reach their zenith in the Cheviot Hills in the east of the area just before the Border swings northwards and descends to the lowlands of the Tweed valley.

During the Second World War a not insignificant number of military aircraft crashed on this high ground. These crashes were perhaps the only way in which the war made any impact on the sparse and isolated rural population, for war or no war, upland farming had to carry on and the reverses of Dunkirk, and Tobruk, the fall of Singapore or the later successes of the victory of El Alamain, the D-Day landings etc. would not stop the lambing or any of the other traditional operations from taking place.

The stories of a number of these crashes have almost achieved folklore status, in particular those that occurred in the Cheviots. Indeed, almost half the aircraft concerned crashed within a confined area around the massif of "The Cheviot" itself. The stories of these aircraft have already been told in a guide entitled "Where the Hills Meet the Sky" and it was while research was being carried out for that guide that stories of other aircraft in the wider Border area began to emerge.

This guide, then, chronicles the stories of the aircraft which crashed in the wider border area but excludes those in the immediate Cheviot area. There is no distinct geographical limit to the area covered by this guide other than it is confined to the border area where Northumberland bounds Scotland and includes an undelineated area each side of that border. Neither does it attempt to be definitive for there is little doubt that some crashes went unrecorded or were poorly recorded by officialdom and that local memories of them have long since gone to the grave along with their owners.

The guide also includes new facts about a few of the events involving some of the aircraft mentioned in "Where the Hills Meet the Sky". This has come about because of overlapping information about incidents included in both guides.

The hill farming and rural community in the area became inextricably involved with these events. It must be remembered that the area was, and is, very sparsely populated and the number of people who would have had first hand knowledge of any crash would therefore be very

7

limited. The passage of time has naturally reduced this number even further, and nowadays the memories of these events are held by a very small band of people indeed. Their memories are, however, quite vivid and reflect the impact that these incidents had on their lives at the time.

The usual words of warning need to be heeded regarding your safety, if, after reading this guide you decide to sally forth and visit the crash sites. You should go well prepared, with plenty of poor weather clothing, for it is an area which affords little shelter from the elements, and the weather can change very rapidly indeed. It is also notoriously difficult to navigate across, especially if you leave a path, because of its total lack of landmarks. You are advised to use 1: 25,000 O.S. maps which show such detail as fence and wall lines rather than the 1:50,000 scale. Much of the area is now afforested and in addition to the entry of woods being frowned on the search for crash sites among the trees is futile. In the unlikely event of you finding a piece of wreckage please leave it where it is for it is a form of memorial to those who may have lost their lives. More than that it still belongs to the Ministry of Defence and its removal is technically stealing. You are particularly warned against touching anything metallic around the Otterburn Military Ranges which form a large part of the area, and into which entry is restricted. Please also remember the Country Code for there are many working farms still in the area and finally make sure that you have told someone where you are going before you set out.

Background

At the start World War II the only military airfield in use close to the Borders and therefore likely to have aircraft flying over it was RAF Acklington. Opened in 1938 it was used as a base for both day and night fighters for much of the war, these fighter squadrons being part of the defence against air attack for the North East. Much further to the south was RAF Unsworth. This was opened in 1930 on the site of a former World War I airfield and although used by operational fighters squadrons during the critical Battle Britain period of 1940 spent much of the rest of the war being used by training units.

As the war progressed the need for aircrew trained to operational standard increased dramatically. As a result of this urgent requirement further airfields were built on the flatter coastal areas to the west and east of the Border Hills. Those built to the East, and forming a horseshoe around the Cheviot Hills, were Ouston, (opened March 1941) Charterhall, (April 1942) Winfield, (April/May 1942) Milfield (August 1942), Brunton (August 1942), Eshott (November 1942) and Boulmer (March 1943). These all became training airfields and all trained fighter pilots. The airfields at Brunton and Winfield were satellites of Milfield and Charterhall respectively. Further to the North, but still to the east of the hills, East Fortune airfield opened in June 1940 as a satellite of the airfield at Drem. It too had once been a WW1 airfield but was reopened in June 1940 to accept some of the airfield at Drem's aircraft movements. It soon became surplus to requirements for that purpose and also became a training airfield.

In the west a further training airfield was established at Crosby-on-Eden, opening in February 1941. Hadrian's Wall formed the northern boundary of this airfield.

All these airfields had fighter Operational Training Units (OTU) based at them. These OTUs were the last stage of a pilots training, and in simple terms taught him how to fly the type of aircraft he would operate once he was posted to an operational squadron. This was a very important stage of a pilot's training as no two types of aircraft have the same flying characteristics and experienced pilots were also retrained at these OTUs when changing to a different type of aircraft. Most OTUs were equipped with aircraft of an earlier Mark of the type than those flown by front-line squadrons. Many of these aircraft had in fact already been operated by front line squadrons and had been released for use by the OTUs when replaced by newer and improved Marks of these aircraft. Because of this previous ownership a substantial number of these aircraft were worn out and of poor serviceability. Indeed many had already been involved in

9

accidents or even suffered damage at the hands of the enemy. The unreliability of these aircraft, together with the inexperience of their pilots was a recipe which gave rise to the frequent accidents which occurred at these OTUs.

But before totally raw pilot got to an OTU he first had to learn basic flying. He did this at an Elementary Flying Training School (EFTS). One of these, 15 EFTS, was based at an airfield known as Kingstown, just to the north of Carlisle. This airfield had been opened in the early 1930s for civilian use. The RAF started to use it in June 1939 and from then until the end of the war it was a very busy training airfield indeed, 108 aircraft being on strength by the end of the war.

Pilots of bomber or transport aircraft were trained in a similar way. First of all taught to fly, and then, as were fighter pilots, given more experience of flying and in-depth training on more powerful and complex aircraft. Having completed this stage of training the pilot then went to a bomber OTU where he would become a member of a crew. All the other members of the crew would have come to the OTU from establishments where they had been being trained in their own particular discipline. There were no bomber OTUs based near the Border area at all but an Air Gunnery School (AGS) was based at RAF Morpeth. This unit, 4 AGS, used the airfield at Tranwell and trained Air Gunners in the skills of trying to shoot down aircraft attacking their own. Navigators, Radio Operators, and Flight Engineers all had their own training facilities and much of this training took place at ground establishments. The aircraft used at bomber OTUs were often the earlier twin engined types such as the Vickers Wellington. By 1943, however, most operational bomber squadrons were either using or converting to the larger four engined aircraft. To operate these aircraft crews had to go through one further level of training. This final phase of training took place at a heavy conversion unit (HCU) and was usually carried out using aircraft of the type which the squadron the trained crew were finally destined for was then operating. These HCUs were most frequently based in the area of Eastern England where the bulk of the operational bomber squadrons were also based. When the four engined heavy bombers were introduced they represented a quantum leap forward in technology. It was the difficulty in establishing the training regime to instruct crews to deal with this new technology which in some way slowed down the entry into the service of these types.

Many British and Commonwealth airmen received their basic initial training, and even sometimes their more advanced training, in Canada under the auspices of the British Commonwealth Air Training Plan (BCATP). This was a scheme entered into by Britain, Canada, Australia, and New Zealand which concentrated training into the open spaces of Canada, and was paid for by Canada (estimated cost $900,000,000). An agreement settling the terms of the plan was signed on 17/12/1939 by the four participating nations. Under the terms of this agreement Britain was to purchase a larger proportion of its wheat requirement from Canada than it had done previously as it's contribution towards the cost of the scheme. More than 131,000 aircrew had been trained in Canada under this plan by the end of hostilities. Some aircrews from 'exiled' European air forces were also trained by this scheme. One other feature of the plan was that it called for squadrons to be formed and staffed on a national basis rather than have squadrons whose personnel were of mixed nationality, although it took some time before this part of the plan was implemented.

The logic behind basing so many fighter OTUs in the area probably lay in the fact that training flights would not hamper operational flights in the far busier Eastern and Southern counties of the United Kingdom. It also lessened the possibility of pilots or a crew under training coming face-to-face with enemy aircraft.

Many bomber OTUs and HCUs had standard training flight routes to the Western and Northern areas of Britain. Once again this was probably to prevent their training overlapping and therefore interfering with operational flights in the busy air space on the eastern side of Britain.

The bombing of Germany, both by day and night, was undertaken by aircraft based mostly in East Anglia, Lincolnshire, the East Midlands and Yorkshire. The RAF carried out most of the night bombing campaign whilst the USAAC (later the USAAF.) was responsible for the day bombing although very early in the war the RAF tried a few daylight bombing raids which on the whole were very unsatisfactory, both in respect of damage done to the targets and also in the losses suffered by the RAF.

Because of this positioning of bomber airfields it became inevitable that some operational aircraft would stray into the Border area. A course which leads from Yorkshire to Southern Germany when extended backwards will cross the Border Area and hence a returning aircraft which on its return from an operational mission failed to find its home airfield would probably continue on and eventually find itself over Northern England or the Borders.

An aircraft could easily fail to find its home airfield for a number of reasons, the chief one being poor visibility due to low cloud or bad weather conditions. Navigation in the air in those days was not an exact science and many of the electronic aids available nowadays did not exist.

The main form of navigation in the air, at least for most of the early years of the war, was a system known as Dead Reckoning. This required the exact ground speed and course to be known and the intervals which elapsed between the changes in these two factors were timed accurately so that a plot of the aircraft's position could be drawn on a chart. The difficulty in this system lay in assessing, accurately, the ground speed and course. The only instruments available to help pilots and navigators in this respect were the airspeed indicator (ASI) and a compass. The ASI recorded the speed through the air, the aircraft's true ground speed being different from this according to the speed and direction of any wind blowing. Similarly, the compass recorded the aircraft's heading but its actual track would be affected by the wind. It was therefore essential that the "wind drift" was calculated very accurately indeed, for an error in that figure would result in an error in the calculated ground speed and course, this in turn resulting in a difference between the aircraft's calculated position and its actual position. In the event that the actual position of an aircraft was in an area of hilly ground but the calculated position showed it to be over relatively low, level ground then the probability of that aircraft striking that hilly ground was greatly increased. This was especially so if visibility was poor and the crew decided to descend so that they could get a glimpse of the ground in order to establish their position.

Early in the war the only "electronic" navigational aid available to aircraft was the Direction Finding Loop (D/F). This equipment consisted, in simple terms, of a radio receiver whose signal was received by an aerial in the form of a loop. This loop was capable of rotation and gave the strongest reception when at 90 degrees to the direction from which the transmission came. So an aircraft could tell its bearings from a ground station (transmitter) and vice versa. If an aircraft got a D/F fix from two ground stations then its position was where these two bearings intersected on the chart. However the D/F. system had a great inherent weakness. It could not distinguish from which side of the aircraft (or ground station) the transmission was coming and it was always possible to calculate two bearings one at 180 degrees (or opposite and technically known as reciprocal) to the other. Quite often the correct bearings could be worked out by logic but sometimes, and not infrequently, it could not. This could often result in the aircraft heading off in exactly the opposite direction to that which would have led it to its intended destination.

Later in the war more sophisticated electronic navigation systems, such as Gee, were developed. They were first introduced as a means of ensuring that the bombers got to their targets accurately and needed a certain amount of skill to operate them. They were soon, however, also used by crews to establish their positions on their return to their home bases but this practice was frowned on by some of the senior officers of Bomber Command. By and large these later electronic

12

navigational systems were complex and a description of their workings is beyond the scope of this guide.

One other method of finding an aircraft's position available to a skilled navigator was an astro-fix. This involved identifying a certain star and then taking bearings off it using a sextant. A very complex calculation was then carried out to establish the aircraft's position. For various reasons this method was not very practicable. For instance an aircraft was often lost because of cloud or poor visibility and in these circumstances a star could probably not be seen either, so precluding the "astro" method of finding its position. Another difficulty was that the aircraft had to be flown on an extremely steady course whilst the "fix" was being taken and this was not always possible or even desirable during a mission over enemy territory.

Difficulties with navigation were not the sole prerogative of allied aircraft. There is little doubt that some of the Luftwaffe aircraft that strayed over the Border area were there because they were lost. There were few strategic targets in the area and any Luftwaffe aircraft flying over it would have either been transiting it whilst en route to one of the larger Scottish or Northern Ireland cities, or simply lost whilst on missions against industrial targets in the Tyneside/Wearside area. Some attacks were also made on coastal towns but any bombs dropped in the deeply rural area of the borders were probably either jettisoned after an aircraft was attacked or lost (or both), or, launched on targets of last resort and opportunity in similar circumstances. The Luftwaffe, too, had radio based navigational aids, one of which was D/F. but early in the war, and certainly before the allies had perfected their first embryonic systems, the Germans used an ingenious system of beams to guide their aircraft to their targets. Amongst these beams were X-Gerat, Y-Gerat and Knickebein and once again the complexities of their workings are beyond the scope of this guide. Suffice it to say that the British defence organisation knew of their existence, and it seems likely that they interfered with these beams in such a way that the German bombers were misled into dropping their weapons on relatively unpopulated areas of no strategic importance. This interference may also have had the effect of confusing the crews, causing them to lose their orientation and stray from an intended course.

Although there were no airfields within the area at the period in time covered by this guide, there was one large military establishment within its bounds. This was and is the Otterburn Ranges. This is a vast tract of open high ground used by the army as a training area, especially for artillery units. Nowadays it is also used as a target area by the RAF but it did not seem to have been used much for this purpose during WWII. On odd occasions, it would seem, Army Co-operation aircraft would join in with exercises taking place on this training area. The area was originally set-aside as an army training establishment just before WWI. It is reputed that Winston Churchill visited the area just before it was handed over to the army. He was the guest at a nearby grouse shoot and apparently passed a comment on what a God forsaken place it was and that the only thing it was fit for was training soldiers. Even at that time Winston was a politician with a considerable amount of influence and within months of his visit the area had been turned over to the army, although whether this was a decision which was influenced by Winston's comment will never be known. During WWI facsimile trench systems were dug on the Ranges in several places and the remnants of these can still be seen to this day.

Virtually the whole of the area was, and is, farmed on an extensive upland basis. The high moorland type of terrain results in mostly poor, unimproved pastures which only support low densities of stock. Most of this stock consists of sheep which are mainly of the hardy hill breeds. For the most part this breed is the Scottish Blackface but further west some of the ewes have Swaledale blood in them and in the extreme west many flocks are pure Swaledale. Although named after the hills in which they were developed there is a lesser number of the whiteheaded and hornless Cheviot breed. Since the war a vast area of the entire region has been planted with trees. This has further reduced the already sparse population. Because of the poor productivity of the ground, large areas of it are needed to create enough income to support viable farm units and therefore the farms tend to be very large indeed in terms of the area they cover. This means that farms tend to be far apart and this in turn results in the wide flung sparsely populated communities. This is perhaps best illustrated by the fact that even today only just over 2,000 people are full-time residents within the boundaries of the Northumberland National Park. Only in the valley bottoms where there is scope to improve the land does the population density rise significantly. Even then there is still little or no arable farming carried out, the improved land, known locally as "in-bye" being used to grow the hay and silage crops necessary to feed the livestock during the often long and bleak winters.

It is not surprising then, given this thinly spread population, that when an aircraft crashed only a few people knew of the incident and were perhaps affected by it. For much the same reason aircraft would be reported as missing and some time elapse before they were found after having crashed. Communications, by today's standards, were also quite poor with only a few farms having the luxury of a telephone and sometimes being at the end of an unmade road. This not only meant that news of a crash was confined to those few people in the area where it occurred but also made it a difficult and slow process to alert the relevant

14

authorities.

All RAF aircraft had, and still have, a serial number. This is a unique and never repeated number consisting of five characters. Early in the war this serial number consisted of one letter plus four digits then became two letters plus three digits as the war progressed, the original series having expired at Z9999. In actuality not all available serial numbers were used. Some had been earmarked for aircraft that were ordered and subsequently never built while others were omitted because they could be easily confused. Instances of the latter are the omission of the letters O, I, and Q from any serial numbers. Some blocks of numbers were also omitted in an attempt to confuse enemy intelligence as to the output of the Allied aircraft industry. Similarly single types of aircraft were never allocated large blocks of serial numbers for a long production run, this once again being an attempt to confuse the enemy. Most aircraft also carried unit code letters. The unit (mostly squadron) code consisted of two letters, although occasionally a figure and a letter were used. So, for instance, 617 Squadron (the Dambusters) had a code AJ. Each individual aircraft then carried another letter of the alphabet, usually separated from the unit code by the RAF roundel, which was that aircraft's identity within the unit. This three-letter code, however, unlike the serial number was not unique. The individual code letters were sometimes changed from aircraft to aircraft within squadrons perhaps due to aircraft becoming unserviceable, or applied to a new aircraft which was replacing one lost on operations or due to an accident. Likewise if a squadron converted to a new type of aircraft then those aircraft would receive the codes carried by the previous type.

Both the Luftwaffe and the USAAF also had a system of serial numbers and unit codes. Luftwaffe aircraft carried a serial number which was a "Werke" number allocated to it by its manufacturer. In the case of some of the manufacturers this "Werke" number included digits which identified the mark of the aircraft. A similar unit code system to the RAF was adopted by the Luftwaffe, although a group of two characters was located either side of the German cross. These two character groups usually consisted of a letter together with a number.

The USAAF serial number was wholly numerical, the first two digits of which represented the year in which the aircraft was ordered. In documentation these two digits were separated from the rest of the number by a hyphen. On the actual aircraft both the first number of the year identifier and the hyphen were frequently omitted so for example 42-56789 became 256789. The unit code system adopted by USAAF was exactly the same as that of the RAF.

RAF aircrews were giving rudimentary survival training,

which included advice and techniques on how to evade capture if forced down in enemy territory. This training also included instructions that if they crashed in a hilly and mountainous area they should move away from the wreck in a downhill direction. On reaching a stream they were further instructed to keep by it and follow it in a downstream direction as this would almost inevitably lead to habitation.

The Aircraft

Several types of aircraft were involved in more than one crash in the Border area and rather than repeat a brief description of these types at the beginning of each of the stories of their particular crashes, these aircraft types are described in this section. These descriptions are very generalised and in no way attempt to give a detailed account of the development, operational use and the history of the type (but see bibliography). Hopefully these notes will help those unfamiliar with WWII aircraft, and apologies are made to those whose knowledge of aircraft is more detailed. When only a single aircraft of a particular type has been involved in a crash a brief description of that type will preface the story of that crash.

At the start of WWII most of the nations involved were operating the first generation of all metal (or mostly all metal) monoplane aircraft with retractable undercarriage. Such was the pace of the development of both airframe and aero engine technology that by early in the war a second generation of this type of aircraft began to enter service. Maximum speeds, rates of climb, service ceiling (the maximum height at which an aircraft will fly), and load carrying capacities all increased by leaps and bounds. These factors, together with the rapid development of airborne electronics (avionics), resulted in aircraft whose ability to strike their targets became ever more predictable and reliable.

Very few military aircraft, of any nation, were the result of private enterprise. Most were designed and built in response to requirements issued by the defence departments of the various governments. In Great Britain the Air Ministry issued specifications to which manufactures then submitted a design. These specifications were identified by a letter and number reference. The letter referred to the type of aircraft required e.g. F. for fighter, while the second of the two numbers was the year in which the specifications was issued with the first number (separated from the second by an oblique) being the count of that particular specification within that year. The inclusion of these specification references in the description of the aircraft gives an insight into the difficulties faced by a government trying to decide how to defend against a perceived and ever changing threat that was some years into the future.

Armstrong — Whitworth Whitley

To the Armstrong — Whitworth Whitley went the distinction of dropping the first British bombs on German soil in WWII. Although an angular, ugly aircraft it had docile flying characteristics, which together with its sturdiness made it a popular aircraft with the crews who flew it. The Whitley was the result of specification B.3/34 calling for a light bomber/ troop transport and Armstrong — Whitworth responded to this requirement in several novel ways. First of all it was its method of construction which employed a stressed skin light alloy monocoque. In order to render the new aircraft simpler to produce the number of component parts was kept to the absolute minimum. Not only that but all the parts were of standard section, and this respect were simplified even further by keeping everything in straight lines and eliminating curves. This later feature also helped reduce the weight of the aircraft. The wing had an unusually thick cross-section which gave it a very high lift capacity. The prototype was powered by two Armstrong — Siddey Tiger IX 14 cylinder radial engines of 795h.p. and first flew on 17/ 03/1936. This was before either the Hampden or Wellington had flown for the first time, both of these aircraft having been the result of a specification issued two years earlier than that issued for the Whitley. This was justification for Armstrong — Whitworth's choice of design and construction. This ease of production also meant that the type entered squadron service very quickly after the first flight of the prototype, in fact in March 1937. This aircraft was the Whitley MkI. It featured, for the first time in a production aircraft, two position variable pitch propellers and a manually operated turret equipped with a with single .303 machine gun in both the nose and tail of the aircraft. Only a few of these aircraft were built, a substitution of the original Tiger engines by a more powerful version of 920 hp resulting in the MkII. A change in the defensive armament with the exchange of the original manually operated nose turret for a Nash and Thomson power operated version equipped with two .303 machine guns resulted in the MkIII. A relatively small number of these two marks were delivered.

Production aircraft up to this point were covered by specification B20/36. A marked improvement in performance, both of maximum speed and rate of climb, resulted from the fitting of Rolls-Royce Merlin engines. This change in power plant plus the substitution of the original rear gun turret by a Nash and Thomson power operated model equipped with four .303 machine gun resulted in the MkIV. This mark was further improved by the substitution of the more powerful Merlin X engines, yielding the MkIVA whilst the fitting further aft by 15 in (37.5 cm) of the rear turret by the simple expedient of lengthening the fuselage, in order to increase that

18

turrets field of fire, resulted in the MkV. Although some MkII's, IVs, and IVA's saw action very early in the war it was the MkV, after entering service early in 1940,which shared the brunt of Bomber Command's early offensive against Germany. It was used against the more distant targets as it had a longer range capability than of either of its two contemporaries, the Wellington and Hampden. Although being replaced in the bomber role by superior four engine type aircraft by late 1941 and early 1942, it was this long-range capability which made it an ideal choice for the ocean and anti-submarine patrols of Coastal Command which it carried out from March 1941. It was improved for this role by the fitting of radar to search for shipping and this version became the MkVII. It was retired from this role in early 1943, having been replaced by more modern and superior types, but continued to serve the RAF, like many obsolescent bomber aircraft, as a transport, and glider tug. Altogether 1,846 Whitleys were built of which over 1400 were MkVs.

Handley-Page Halifax

The Halifax has never received the attention and acclaim enjoyed by the Lancaster whose illustrious career tended to overshadow it. This is a pity for although having a shaky start it developed into a very competent aircraft, not only dropping an equal tonnage of bombs on Germany as the Lancaster but also being used as a glider tug and transport.

It was Air Ministry specification B1/35 for a twin engined heavy bomber with a wing span not exceeding a hundred feet which prompted the initiation of the design by Handley — Page which finally became the Halifax. Before this design, the HP55, was complete the Air Ministry issued another two specifications, B12/36, which resulted in the Short Stirling and P13/36 which spawned, via the Manchester, the Lancaster. Both of these specifications influenced the Handley — Page design team, and finally the HP56 design, a development of the HP 55, was drawn up to meet specification P13/36. Like the Manchester this aircraft was to utilise two Rolls-Royce Vulture engines, which were still under development. However in July 1937 it was decided that insufficient Vulture engines would be available for both the Manchester and the HP 56 and the design was altered yet again to be powered by four Rolls-Royce Merlin engines, this new design receiving the type number HP57. With the benefit of hindsight this was a fortuitous decision for the Halifax, as the Vulture turned out to be a very poor and unreliable engine indeed. Other engine types were also considered at this time but it was with four Merlins that the prototype first took to the air on 25/10/1939. It entered squadron service with 35 Squadron at RAF Leeming in November 1940 and carried out its first operational mission in March 1941. This was the Halifax MkI and as experience was gained in its use it soon became clear that the type had some serious shortcomings. In particular both the performance and handling characteristics left something to be desired. The lack of performance was attributed to the drag caused by the front gun turret and as it became recognised that very few frontal attacks were carried out by Luftwaffe night fighters this was deleted and replaced by a more streamlined nose shortly after the MkII entered production. The MkII had more powerful Merlin engines and initially was fitted with a dorsal turret. The original type of dorsal turret also induced a considerable amount of drag, and several different types were tried before the best balance between defensive firepower and performance-sapping drag was found. But a more serious problem was the Halifax's tendency to go into an uncontrollable and usually terminal spin without warning. This was traced to an aerodynamic problem with the fins and rudders. Eventually a new design of this feature was introduced and this was incorporated in the production line and the MkII, and MkVs both acquired this new fin design. The MkV was a MkII fitted with a different type of undercarriage, this having been necessitated by a shortage of the original design of undercarriage. Some older aircraft were retroactively fitted with the new type of fin when they became due for major overhauls.

The Merlin engines fitted to Halifax, rather uncharacteristically, had also been causing problems, in that they had a tendency to overheat, and in some cases engines had caught fire. It was decided to re-engine the aircraft with air cooled engines in an attempt to overcome this problem. The engine chosen was the Bristol Hercules 14 cylinder radial. When this engine was installed, together with the new design of fin, the Halifax was transformed, this version becoming the MkIII. Although later Marks were introduced (MkVI and VIII) these were basically derived from the MkIII and it was this Mark that was by far away the most numerous of all the Marks of the Halifax. The MkIII first entered Squadron service in February 1944. Altogether 6,176 Halifax's were built of which just over 2,000 were MkIII and 1,900, MkIIs.

Not all these aircraft, however, were built by Handley Page. They were also built by Fairey Aviation, English Electric, Rootes Securities and the London Aircraft Production Group, which utilised the facilities and personnel of London Transport's bus repair depots.

Hawker Hurricane

Just as the Halifax was overshadowed by the Lancaster, the Hawker Hurricane was eclipsed by its more illustrious contemporary, the

Spitfire. This is also a pity for it was a fine aircraft which, contrary to popular belief, bore the brunt of air defence of Britain during the early stages of the war. In fact during the Battle of Britain there were almost twice as many Hurricanes as there were Spitfires and Fighter Command's only recipient of the Victoria Cross was a Hurricane pilot, F/Lt J.B. Nicholson of 249 Squadron.

Originally designed by Sydney Camm to meet Air Ministry specification F6/34 the Hurricane was a logical development of Hawker's earlier single engined biplane fighters. The prototype first flew in 1936 powered by the first version of the Rolls-Royce Merlin V-12 engine, which itself became a legend by powering some of the most successful and charismatic aircraft of WWII. The prototype proved to be a great success, being both exceptionally fast and very manoeuvrable. It entered squadron service in 1938 and served throughout the war in all theatres.

Although built in large numbers, 14,000 being produced, only a few marks of the Hurricane were developed the basic difference between them being the use of more powerful versions of the Merlin engines. Another difference was the substitution of the canvas covering of the earlier marks by aluminium alloy sheeting. The Mark X was a version of the Mark II produced in Canada.

The Hurricane lent itself easily to adaptation and as it's role as an air defence fighter diminished it was increasingly used as a ground attack bomber (fighter — bomber) and when equipped with a large calibre cannon was used as a tank buster.

It also the first aircraft type to use rocket projectiles operationally. Incidentally, one of the first squadrons equipped with this type of Hurricane, 164 Squadron, carried out its initial training with these rockets while based at RAF Milfield in early 1943.

The Hurricane had several features which endeared it to its pilots. One was its wide- track undercarriage which made landing a relatively easy operation especially when compared to the Spitfire. It could also absorb a considerable amount of battle damage before it became unflyable. Not only that, but the early fabric covered aircraft could be repaired very quickly and easily indeed.

All in all, then, the Hurricane was a good all round aircraft which perhaps tends, nowadays, to get less than its fair share of accolades.

Vickers Wellington

The Wellington was designed and built in response to Air Ministry specification B.9/32. It was designed by Sir Barnes Wallis who later achieved lasting fame as the designer of the bouncing bomb used by the "Dambusters". This specification also gave rise to the Handley-Page Hampden which together with the Whitley and Wellington bore the brunt of RAF Bomber Command's early offensive against Germany. However, the design of the Wellington tried to achieve the opposite end of the spectrum of performance requirements to that of the Hampden. Whereas the Hampden would, it was hoped, deliver a moderate bomb load at high speed, the Wellington would deliver a heavier bomb load, at lower speed and at a greater distance.

The Vickers design team, headed by Barnes Wallis, decided to adopt a novel method of construction first used in the R100 airship known as geodetic. This employed thin alloy strips woven in an almost basket like way, the forces in adjoining strips being directed in such a way that they cancel each other out. This gave an immensely strong stress free structure which was extremely light. This later feature was enhanced by the whole aircraft being fabric covered. A prototype, known as the Vickers Type 271 was first flown on 15/06/1936. The Air Ministry was so impressed with this aircraft that a different specification B29/36 was drawn up to cover production aircraft. The first production Wellington first flew on 23/12/1937 and differed considerably from the type 271. It had, like the type 271, a deep, portly, streamlined fuselage which later gave rise to its affectionate nickname of "Wimpy" after Popeye's obese friend J. Wellington Wimpy. It was powered by two Bristol Pegasus nine cylinder radial engines each of 950 h.p. The shape of the wings was also unusual in that they were of high aspect ratio. This is the ratio between the width and length of wing and when this figure is high it confers an improved high altitude performance on the aircraft. The fitting of power operated twin machine gun turrets in both the nose and tail of the new aircraft was also an innovation. In early aircraft these turrets were built by Vickers themselves with the controls provided by Fraser -Nash. In aircraft manufactured from 1939 onwards these turrets were replaced by hydraulic versions provided by Nash and Thompson.

It was believed that these turrets would be able to deliver such a weight of firepower that a formation of aircraft so equipped could produce a field of fire which would render them immune from attack by defending fighters. When eventually put to the test this theory proved to be disastrously wrong, large numbers of Wellington's being lost to enemy fighters in early attempts at daylight bombing.

When tactics were changed the Wellington found it's true niche as a night bomber.

It had first entered Squadron service in 1938 and continued to serve up till and beyond the end of the war. It was replaced as a night bomber by the later four engined types from 1942 — 43 onwards but

22

continued to serve in Coastal Command as an anti-submarine and ocean patrol aircraft and also as a training aircraft. It also served as a medium bomber until the end of the war in some overseas theatres of operations. Improved marks continued to be developed throughout the war and several different types of engine were tried. Perhaps the most successful of these was the Bristol Hercules XI which powered the Mark III, Mark VIII, Mark X and several later Marks.

The Wellington was liked and trusted by the crews who flew it. It was a reliable aircraft with few flying vices and had an enviable reputation for the amount of damage it could suffer and still return home. One of its few drawbacks was that in the unfortunate circumstance of having to make a crash landing the Wellington had a propensity to catch fire. This was caused by the location of a fuel tank behind each engine and in the event of a crash these usually spilt high-octane fuel which then surged forward over the red-hot engines with a fire being the inevitable result. Nevertheless, the Wellington was one of those aircraft which formed the backbone of the RAF during the war years, and altogether over 14,000 were produced.

The Aircraft Engines

The vast steps forward in aircraft performance which occurred during the late 1930s and WWII would not have been possible without a similar and simultaneous increase in the performance of aero-engines.

The reasons for this increase are many and varied and are of such a technical nature to take them beyond the scope of this guide. But briefly, and in a generalised view, then better materials for construction, high-pressure supercharging, variable pitch propellers and the development of high octane petrol must rank amongst those factors having the greatest influence on this performance increase.

Unlike the aircraft, aero engines were usually designed as a private venture, and this required a high degree of resolve on behalf of the manufacturer because although a large amount of money could be spent on developing a new engine no sales for it could be guaranteed.

Many of the aircraft types described in this guide were powered by just a few types of aero engine and these engines are worthy of a brief description in that not only is mention made of them time and time again, but also because of their importance to the success of several types of aircraft.

Perhaps the most notable of these engines was the Rolls-Royce Merlin. This very successful engine powered many of the most important types of British aircraft including the Spitfire, Hurricane, Lancaster, Mosquito etc etc and also the Mustang (or P- 51), an American aircraft.

The Rolls-Royce Merlin was a 12 cylinder liquid cooled piston engine with two banks of six cylinders arranged in a "V" configuration on the crankcase. It followed a long line of Rolls-Royce engines of similar configuration but contrary to popular belief it was not a development of the engine which powered the Schneider Trophy winning Supermarine S6B seaplane. Although benefiting from some of the development work done for this engine the Merlin was a totally new design and the first prototype ran for the first time in October 1933. Development of the engine, however, was not without its problems and several redesigns of the cylinder blocks and heads had to be undertaken before the engine became reliable. The first reliable production version came off the production line in November 1936. As the promise of this new engine became apparent more aircraft designers chose it to power their aircraft and in turn asked for higher power outputs. Throughout the war Rolls-Royce engineers responded to this call for more and more power. This was achieved by ever increasing degrees of supercharging. The original version of the Merlin had a single stage, single speed supercharger whilst the versions produced at the war's end had two speed, two stage superchargers. In simple terms this higher degree of supercharging meant that more air was forced into the engines, thereby allowing more fuel to be burnt with a resulting increase in power. Various detailed design changes were made throughout the war to improve the engine's reliability and the Merlin was license built in the UK by the Ford Motor Co. and in the USA by Packard. Altogether 168,000 Merlin engines were built, making it the most numerous piston aero engine ever built.

But almost equally important to the British aircraft industry were the radial, air-cooled engines produced by the Bristol Aeroplane Company. This group of engines further sub divides into those equipped with poppet valves and those having sleeve valves. The differences between these two types of valve are very technical and, once again beyond the scope of this guide, except to point out that a poppet valve is the type of valve used in modern vehicle engines. The poppet valve engines, the Mercury and Pegasus, were both nine cylinder single row engines.

The Mercury was a development of the Jupiter engine, itself designed by Bristol Chief designer Roy Fedden just after WWI. The first Mercury was built and ran in 1926 and produced 800 h.p. This was a racing engine and subsequent production engines produced 400 to 500 h.p. The engine continued to be developed right through the 1930s into the early 1940s and later versions, with supercharges were producing 820 h.p. The most noteworthy operational aircraft using this engine was the Bristol Blenheim. The Pegasus was in fact a Mercury with a longer cylinder stroke and the first version of 550 h.p. initially ran in 1932. It went on, with modification and the addition of superchargers, to develop 1,000 h.p. by 1938. It was used in several types of aircraft which were important at the start of the war including the Wellington and Handley-Page Hampden, and also the Short Sunderland flying boat, which was important throughout the whole war.

The sleeve valve engines included the Perseus, a single row nine cylinder engine and the Taurus and Hercules, which were both two row 14 cylinder engines. Although both the Perseus and the Taurus were successful and reliable engines neither were built in large quantities as they powered only a few types of less well-known and successful aircraft. The only type of aircraft in RAF service to utilise the Perseus was the Blackburn Botha and similarly the Taurus only powered the Bristol Beaufort and Fairey Albacore, both of which were torpedo bombers. However the Hercules was built in large numbers and arguably was just as important to Britain's war effort as was the Rolls-Royce Merlin. The earliest version, first ran in 1936, producing 1,150 h.p. but by 1938, the Hercules was producing 1,375 h.p. Continued development, mostly in the form of changes to supercharger gearing and impeller sizes, ensured that the engine was producing nearly 1,700 h.p. by 1941. It was chosen to power, and did so with great success, several important and accomplished aircraft types. These include the Bristol Beaufighter, several Marks of the Vickers Wellington, the Short Stirling, the most successful Marks of the Handley-Page Halifax (i.e. Marks III, VI, and VIII) and even one Mark of the Avro Lancaster. It became liked for its great reliability and by the end of the war could run for 2,000 hours between major overhauls. Over 57,000 Hercules engines were produced during the war. It continued to be built into the mid-1950s to power the first generation of post-war civilian passenger aircraft, where once again it gained an enviable reputation for its reliability and low maintenance downtime.

The Events

This section chronicles the circumstances of each crash. The descriptions attempt to detail information such as where the aircraft had taken off from, its unit, the name(s) of the pilot or crew, the reason for it being over the Border Hills, the exact place of crash, and how the local community became involved in each crash. Unfortunately this information is not available on a uniform basis for each crash and it is therefore inevitable that there appear to be inconsistencies in the depth of detail of the stories.

Bristol Blenheim I K7067 30/08/1938

This incident occurred before the start of World War II and it is therefore not strictly within the remit of this guide. It is included, however, because both the type of aircraft involved, and one of its crew went on to serve the RAF with distinction in the early years of the war.

When the Bristol Blenheim first made its debut in 1936 it was considered to be a revolution in aircraft design. It was the first all metal monoplane of stressed skin construction to be placed in production for the RAF and it stemmed from design work carried out for a proposed high-speed commercial aircraft in 1934. Lord Rothermere, the newspaper magnate, had become interested in the project which was known as the Bristol 142. This aircraft was eventually built as a private project with financial help from Lord Rothermere, and flew for the first time in April 1935. It was a twin engined medium-sized aircraft and its performance exceeded all expectations. By June 1935 it was undergoing trials at the A and AEE based at Martlesham Heath. These trials showed that the aircraft had a maximum speed of 285m.p.h. which was 30 m.p.h. faster than the Gloucester Gladiator, the latest fighter entering service with the RAF. So impressed were RAF with the aircraft that they asked Lord Rothmere for permission to carry out further trials. He bettered their request by giving them the aircraft naming it "Britain First" when he did so. Within a short space of time the Air Ministry issued a specification, B28/35, covering a modified Type 142 which went on to become the Blenheim. The first production aircraft (K 7033) also served as a trials aircraft, there being no prototype, and flew for the first time on 25/06/1936. The trials proved a great success and Bristol were instructed by the Air Ministry to get the aircraft into full production with all possible speed. A year later 24 Blenheims a month were being built and the Mark I version entered

26

service with 114 Squadron in March 1937. This version was powered by two Bristol Mercury engines of 840 hp and achieved a maximum speed of 280 m.p.h at its best operational altitude. This startling performance was considered to be sufficient defence against fighters and consequently little defensive armour was deemed necessary. The flaw in this piece of logic was that the very same technology which had produced the startling performance of the Blenheim was not only available to but also made use of by the designers and manufacturers of fighter aircraft. Although the Mk I Blenheim had been replaced by the Mk IV by the start of the war its reliance on performance rather than defensive armament led to the type suffering heavy losses at the hands of fighters in the early stages of the war and before it was replaced by superior types. Perversely, perhaps, many of the redundant and obsolete Mk I bombers were converted to night fighters (Mark IF) in which roll they were reasonably successful, and one in which

they had a claim to fame in that they became the first aircraft in the world to be equipped with airbourne radar for detecting their prey.

K 7067 was among the first 30 or so Blenheims off the production line. It was issued to 90 Squadron, based at RAF Bicester, on 23/07/1937. It subsequently became the 500 hour development aircraft for that Squadron.

On Tuesday 30/08/1938 K 7067 took off from Bicester on a cross-country training flight. It was piloted by an Australian, F/O H.I. Edwards, the 'A' Flight commander, with Sgt W.F. Nash as Observer and AC 1 J.A. Theoplilus as Wireless Operator. The time of takeoff is not recorded but by referring to subsequent events was probably in late mid-morning. The number of

W/C H.I. Edwards, pilot of Blenheim K7067

27

training flights had increased substantially at the time because of the heightened state of readiness of the RAF caused by the tension of the Munich Crisis. No details of the route of the flight are known but eventually the aircraft arrived over the Otterburn Range. It is unlikely that they was any military significance in this and certainly no mention is made of the aircraft being on some kind of joint exercise with the army. It was, therefore, much more likely that it was pure coincidence which led it to be over the Army Training Area when it started to experience difficulties due to icing. This is a condition when, because of the prevailing weather conditions, ice starts to form on the surface of the aircraft. Once started the process accelerates rapidly with the result that not only does the aircraft's weight increase but its carefully proportioned aerodynamic shapes begin to alter. This results not only in an increase in drag but also a reduction in lift. Inevitably there comes a point when the increased weight of the aircraft can no longer be supported by the reducing lift and the aircraft simply ceases to fly. F/O Edwards must have judged this point to be close and he and the other two members of the crew abandoned the aircraft by parachute.

That the aircraft was in difficulties had been seen by the Rogerson family at Cottonshope Farm. The relief they must have felt on seeing the parachutes blossom out from the aircraft was, however, short lived. Two of parachutes opened out and started to float down normally but the third parachute canopy fouled the tail fin of the now rapidly plummeting Blenheim and became entangled on it. The unfortunate occupant of this parachute's harness was now being dragged through the air astern of the stricken aircraft. Very fortunately indeed the parachutes canopy slipped away from the aircraft fin, but only shortly before the aircraft impacted on the ground and thus did not have enough time to deploy correctly. It had not checked the speed of the fall of the airmen attached to it, who was in fact the pilot, F/O Edwards, and he hit the ground at what would normally have been a fatal speed. But fortunately, fate smiled on him, for he was in a vertical position and the spot where he made his landfall was very soft peat. This was just a few yards south of the fence line which ran east about 300m from Cottonshope at OS grid ref NT 793046. When the Rogerson family got to him F/O Edwards was embedded in the peat up to his arm pits. Almost simultaneously the aircraft had crashed about 200 metres south of F/O Edward's landfall, destroying about 60 metres of drystone walling as it did so. The occupants of the other two parachutes landed reasonably safely, one on the flat topped hill to the north west of Cottonshope known as Pepperside and the other on White Kip a prominent height on a ridge called Loan Edge to the east of Cottonshope. Sgt. Nash suffered slight injuries to a knee whilst ACI

28

Theoplilus dislocated his neck.

F/O Edwards had to be dug out of the peat, and great care had to be exercised to ensure that his injuries were not exacerbated by his extraction from it.His injuries, to legs and head, were fairly severe and it was sometime before he got back to flying. But get back he did, and with a vengeance, for he was to have an illustrious career in the RAF in the early stages of WW II.

At the time of the accident F/O Edwards had 424 hours of flying in his log book of which 183 had been spent flying Blenheims. K7067 had completed 352.20 hours of flying when its service with the RAF came to an abrupt end.

Although the Blenheim never lived up to the, perhaps, over ambitious expectations of it, it did, in its later Marks, carry out at significant number of successful operations against the enemy. Sadly, though, most of these operations resulted in a large number of Blenheims and their crews being lost. It ceased to be used operationally in August 1942 in the European theatre of war and at the end of 1943 in the Middle and Far East.

Armstrong Whitworth Whitley V P4952, 15/10/1940

When the slabsided and ugly Whitley V, P4952, coded ZA-R of 10 Squadron took off from RAF Leeming on the evening of 14/10/1940 it was not the first time that the crew captained by S./L. K. F.Ferguson had flown together. Alongside S/L Ferguson were his 2nd pilot, Sergeant Rogers, Observer, Sergeant Fraser, Wireless Operator, Sergeant Cummings and Air gunner, Sergeant Niman. They had flown together on several occasions before and on 24/08/1940 they had flown in the same aircraft, P4952, on a mission to Milan. P4952 was in fact a veteran of at least 19 missions (see Appendix 1 for details of operations by both aircraft and crew). It had been allocated to 10 Squadron on 01/05/1940 after having been delivered initially to 9 MU on 06/04/1940 for the fitting of some unspecified equipment. The aircraft seems to have been flown on most occasions by a crew captained by F/O Prior, but had, just after its allocation to the Squadron, been flown on three missions by W/C Staton, the squadron CO. Only a month earlier on 14/09/1940 S/L. Ferguson's crew had been briefed to take part in an attack on the invasion barges in Antwerp harbour. However, shortly after take-off their Whitley, P4966 had developed engine trouble over the North Sea. The decision was made to "ditch" the aircraft and S./L Ferguson made an excellent "landing" about twenty miles east off Spurn Head. All the crew got clear of the

Whitley crew captained by Sgt. Hickling. Sgt. Mark Niman is on extreme right of picture. Sgt. Hickling is 4th figure from left.

aircraft safely and into the dinghy within minutes. This was just as well for the aircraft sank after only 15 minutes. The crew of another 10 Squadron aircraft from Leeming, flown by Sergeant Willis, had spotted the flares sent up by the ditched crew. They reported the dinghy's position and five hours later S/L. Ferguson and his crew were picked up by the 200-ton mine sweeper H.M.S. Kurd. This vessel continued with its mine sweeping task before delivering the "ditched" crew to Grimsby.

Now, perhaps even more united as a crew by this previous adversity, they were to take part in another highly dangerous mission. Along with 7 other aircraft of 10 Squadron they had been detailed to attack a synthetic oil refinery at Stettin(Scezin). This meant a long flight over enemy territory with all the attendant risks which that carried with it. Having taken off between 17:25 and 17:40 hours the omens for the success of the mission did not appear to bode well when one of the aircraft dispatched, Whitley P4993, crashed near Weybridge after becoming entangled in barrage balloon cables. The crew, captained by Sergeant Wright, were unfortunately all killed.

However, despite this setback and deteriorating weather conditions the remaining aircraft persevered with their mission and successfully attacked the target with little opposition from its defenders. Because of the ever deteriorating weather conditions and the length of

30

time the aircraft had been airborne they were contacted at 0240 hours on 15/10/1940 and instructed to land at RAF Marham in Norfolk. Aircraft C, J, Z, and S., acknowledged this message by 0300 hours but nothing was heard from the other aircraft. These two aircraft were now running short of fuel and at 0430 hours, the crew of T4143 were ordered to bale out. However, two of them failed to do so, and were subsequently killed when the aircraft crashed near Thirsk.

Still no recorded contact had been made between Leeming and P4952 and its crew. Sgt Niman the tail gunner, who was also trained as wireless operator recalls, however, that a message was received instructing them to divert and land at RAF Marham. This message was received and acknowledged with the response that the aircraft's position was just north of Hexham and that insufficient fuel remained to reach either the diversion airfield or Leeming. Further instructions were received by the crew that they should climb to 8,000 feet put the aircraft on an easterly course (i.e. towards the sea) and then abandon it. None of this radio traffic is recorded by either 10 Squadron's or Leeming's Operational Record Books, the first contact with S/L Ferguson being recorded as having been made at 0900 hours, approximately four hours after the abandonment of the aircraft. However, the radio log at RAF Topcliffe confirmed that these messages had been transmitted.

On receiving the orders to abandon the aircraft the crew did precisely that. The tail gunner, Sergeant Mark Niman, got out of his turret and made his way to the escape hatch at the front of the aircraft, donning his parachute as he went. He dangled his body through the hatch with only elbows retaining him. By quickly drawing his elbows together he jettisoned himself from the fuselage and once clear of the aircraft pulled the rip-cord. To his relief the parachute opened and he found himself above the cloud layer. He realised that it would be some time before he reached the ground and decided that it would be an excellent opportunity, while he had some height, to try out some of the things he had been taught in training regarding manoeuvring the 'chute'. After all he wanted to avoid tall trees and church steeples at all costs. He had been told that a tug on the right hand parachute lines would result in a move to the right while the opposite effect would result from a tug on the left hand lines. He tried this and immediately regretted having done so, for it set up a violent pendulum movement which made him very sick. Sgt Niman was now in the cloud and fog, and so, despite there being a full moon, could not judge where the ground was. There was little point therefore, on adopting the relaxed landing position he had been taught. In the eventuality he made a good landing. He could not see anything of his surroundings and as it was rather cold he wrapped himself in the parachute canopy and went off to sleep.

At daybreak he woke and started to make his way to a landmark, possibly a tree, which he could see in the distance. Just as he approached it he was 'captured' by a group of Homeguard armed with pitchforks. Despite his protestations he was marched off to the nearest police station. This was probably Bellingham as it was from there that the message was received at Leeming telling of the safety of the crew, and in any case police stations in remote Northumberland , were, and are, few and far between and certainly the one in Bellingham would have been the nearest to the site of the eventual crash of the aircraft. The rest of the crew, who had arrived at the police station , were also being treated with utmost suspicion. Perhaps the propaganda regarding the trustworthiness of anyone who came out of the sky on a parachute had been a little too successful! A local large scale land owner, described by Sgt Niman as "the Squire", then arrived on the scene and quickly cleared up the identity of the crew. Having once confirmed this, he took the crew to a mansion where they were treated to a grouse dinner. The identity of this large house cannot now be established, although there is a strong possibility that it may have been Nunick Hall.

Eventually transport arrived from Leeming and the crew were taken back there, apparently unharmed by their experience. They were returned to operational flying within days.

Having finally run out of fuel P4952 plunged from the sky and at approximately 05:00 hrs crashed on some open moorland belonging to Brieredge Farm, a few miles south of Bellingham. It remained remarkably intact and faced in a south westerly direction. No guard was put in place to protect it and more than two weeks elapsed before work was commenced on removing it. During this time the crashed aircraft was visited on a regular basis by a number of local young boys, including 12 year old 'Tommy' Thompson. He vividly remembers that because of the lack of a guard at the aircraft they were able to remove many pieces from it, including the radio (or parts of it). These were prized possessions. The crash site has previously been quoted as being Watch Crags but is actually probably closer to both Bell Crag and Meslin Crags, and lies slightly east of a line between these two points. Any local recall of the crash inevitably refers to the "Meslin Aeroplane", confirming the site of P4952's final resting-place.

Opposite page - Operational crew of 10 Squadron, RAF in September 1940.
Sgt. Dove is 3rd from left on second row. Sgt. Niman is 6th from right on the 3rd row.

Armstrong Whitworth Whitley V P4957 30/10/40

Only two weeks were to elapse after the demise of P4952 before the transport pool of Leeming was once again called on to collect the crew of a crashed aircraft from the Border area. Once again the aircraft, Whitley V serial no. P4957 was operated by 10 Squadron.

It is not generally appreciated that by October 1940 Bomber Command's campaign against Germany was already up and running and a significant number of missions had already been carried out although, of course, the number of aircraft committed to a raid was very small when compared to the better known huge attacks carried out later in the war. Very few aircraft, comparatively, were available and they were flown by a small number of squadrons and this meant these squadrons were already flying missions on a disproportionately busy and regular basis. 10 Squadron was one of those units and since the German invasion of the Low Countries in May they had been used to bomb enemy targets on an increasingly regular basis. So much so that some of its aircrew were already completing a "tour" (30 missions). At this stage these aircrew would be stood down (later known as "screened") from operational flying

Crew of Whitley P4957(ZA-E) outside Alston Cottage Hospital immediately after crash. L to R - Sgt. George, Sgt. Miner, Nurse Thompson, P/O Peers, Sgt. Ottway, Sgt, Dove.

34

and transferred to training units where they would be used to instruct fledgling aircrew. One such man was Sgt. George Dove.

Sgt Dove had joined the RAF in 1938 at the age of 17 and had been trained as a wireless operator. He had already completed 30 missions when, on 29/10/1940, he was asked to undertake an extra one. The concept of regular crews, of permanent composition, always flying the same aircraft (serviceability allowing) had only begun to be adopted and Sgt Dove had flown with eight different captains whilst completing his 30 missions. The crew he had been detailed to join did however seem to have

View looking South of the general area of the crash site of Whitley P4957(ZA-E).

been a little more stable. The Captain, P/O Peers, together with 2nd Pilot Sgt Ottway, Observer (Navigator) Sgt George, Air Gunner Sgt Miner and Wireless Operator Sgt Matthews had flown 7 previous missions together, but for this mission to Wilhemshaven on 29/10/1940 Sgt Matthews was replaced by Sgt Dove. The aircraft they were to fly that night, Whitley P4957, coded ZA-E, had been flown by them on 5 of these missions, so it had almost become their regular aircraft. (See Appendix II for operational history of aircraft and crew).

Along with another aircraft of 10 squadron they were detailed to attack the docks and shipbuilding facilities at Wilhelmshaven on the north coast of Germany. In addition four other aircraft from 10 Squadron were briefed to attack a synthetic oil refinery at Magdeburg. All the aircraft took off in rapid succession between 1656 and 1701 hours. ZA-E and its crew arrived over Wilhelmshaven without mishap and successfully dropped

35

their bombs on the docks as briefed. Aircraft from 10 Squadron had already visited Wilhelmshaven on several previous occasions and had found it to be a strenuously defended target. The night of 29/10/1940 proved to be no different and there was considerable searchlight activity together with intense anti-aircraft gunfire. However, ZA-E and its crew remained unscathed and started on their homeward journey. This proved uneventful. Uneventful, that is, until they arrived in the circuit to land at Leeming. This was at 2300 hours. Earlier that evening, at 1830 hrs. Leeming had been attacked by an enemy aircraft believed to have been a Junkers 88. Nerves at Leeming must have been a little on edge that night because when P/O Peers asked for permission to land he was told to fly away from the area because of the possibility of enemy aircraft still being in the area, although the Operations Record show that he was given permission to land after he had circled the airfield several times. The aircraft did not land and subsequently headed off in the direction of Barnard Castle. The aircraft carried on in a north-westerly direction and was tracked by RAF Catterick to the vicinity of Appleby, Westmoreland (now Cumbria). It was a night of thick cloud and heavy rain. About 20 minutes after turning away from Leeming P/O Peers asked Sgt Dove to obtain a radio bearing (known in flying terms as a QDM) from Leeming. Sgt Dove did so and passed the information on to his pilot. Very shortly afterwards P/O Peers asked for another QDM. On receipt of this one he expressed some doubt as to its accuracy and said that he would turn on to its reciprocal course (the exactly opposite direction) as it appeared that they were not getting any closer to base.

As the aircraft banked into the turn there was an enormous bang on the starboard wing and the cockpit started to fill with smoke. P/O Peers looked at the instruments and saw that they were at 2,000 feet. He assumed that they had hit a barrage balloon cable and ordered the crew to bale out. Sgt Dove donned his parachute and started to make his way back down the fuselage to the exit door. As he put his hand on the handle to open it there was another huge crash and he was hurled back to the main spar. For what seemed an eternity there was crashing and tearing sounds while Sgt Dove desperately tried to cling on to something but to little avail. In fact this phase only lasted a few seconds and then all went absolutely silent. Sgt Dove made his way back to the door once again and this time stepped out into the pouring rain and on to long tussocky grass. It was pitch dark and almost exactly midnight. (Records show the crash as having occurred at 0012 on 30/10/1940 at 2500 ft a.s.l.) Sgt Dove then heard voices and one by one he was joined by the rest of the crew. At first they thought the aircraft might burst into flames, but when, after some time it had not they decided to climb back into it to shelter from the rain. Sgt Dove was alone in having suffered some slight injuries to his left arm, the rest of the crew remaining unharmed. His injuries were treated with the aircraft "First Aid" kit and they then consumed what remained of the coffee and flying rations. They had received a severe shaking and because of this could not sleep and for the remainder of the night just chatted with one another and dozed fitfully.

When the cold light of dawn finally came they could see that they were high up on the "Pennines". Their aircraft had apparently flown between the two ridges of hills which formed the east and west sides of the River South Tyne Valley. The first bang had been the starboard wing striking the tip of the western ridge, the subsequent crashing and tearing resulting from the aircraft again making contact with the ground and sliding down the descending slope. As it came to a halt it slewed through 180^0. It's final resting place was on a finger of fellside which jutted out between the two steep sided gorges of the Gelt Burn and one of its tributaries. There was an 80 foot precipitous drop between where the aircraft had finally come to rest and the bottom of these clefts. This location is about 2 to 3 miles to the south west of Slaggyford. The navigator, Sgt George, set off to try and find help. He had not been gone very long when the shepherd of the nearest farm, the Knar, stumbled across them. True to hill shepherding tradition Robert Turnbull was carrying a flask of whisky (its efficacy in reviving newly born lambs is questionable, but it has a wonderful effect on tired and cold shepherds!!) and offered all the crew a nip. At that moment they noticed a line of figures advancing over the distant fell top, and on looking in the opposite direction they saw another line of figures approaching them. Because the crash had occurred so close to the Cumberland/Northumberland border both counties' police forces had been alerted when The Royal Observer Corps had reported the crash. These police were now drawing near to the crashed aircraft and were guided to it by the crew firing off a "Verey" cartridge.

As the police started to escort the crew to their waiting cars the navigator returned. He was rather upset because on knocking on the door of the first farmstead he had come to, he had been confronted with a shotgun. Once again, like Sgt Niman, he had to convince the occupants that he was not a "Luftwaffe airman". This farmstead was probably the Knar but may have been Far House.

The police had probably left their cars in the village of Slaggyford, as it was from there at 1030, that Leeming had been informed of the crash and of the survival of the crew.

The crew were taken to the "Cottage Hospital" at Alston where Sgt Dove's injuries were tended to and the rest of the crew given a medical check. As transport could not be arranged for that day the crew were billeted out with local families, Sgt Dove spending the night with the local doctor. The following day transport arrived from Leeming and finally the crew of ZA-E arrived back at their base after nearly 2 arduous days.

Inevitably questions were asked as to what had happened and why, and initially a finger of suspicion was pointed in the direction of the accuracy of Sgt Dove's radio reception techniques. Fortunately he had retained his radio log and when checked against the log of the D/F unit at Leeming it was found that he had been given a QDR (a reciprocal course) and not a QDM. The D/F operator had made the mistake and he was subsequently put on a charge. It did mean of course, that ZA-E had been flying in exactly the opposite direction to that intended and this, together with the poor weather conditions, had resulted in it striking the fellside. Had the aircraft been five feet lower it would probably have hit the hill head on with a resulting crash of a very violent nature. But Lady Luck had been smiling and the crew had been very fortunate indeed.

Vickers Wellington Ic   T2546   30/10/1940

Wellington T2546 crashed just in front of the small, dark wood on the first ridge of hills - Dargues Hope Farm in the valley in the nearer foreground.

Closer view of crash site of Wellington T2546 - site is on field boundary running from small dark wood towards the camera, and about 100m from that wood.

Within minutes of Whitley ZA-E of 10 Squadron crashing into the hillside above Slaggyford, a Wellington Ic, T2546 coded VF-A of 99 Squadron met a similar fate 25 miles or so to the north-east.

T2546 was a relatively new aircraft when it took off for a raid on Berlin on the 29/10/1940. A description of the aircraft is included in Chapter Two. It had first been issued to 23 MU on the 30/06/1940, but over 2 months elapsed before it was finally allocated to a squadron. The first recipient of the new aircraft was 9 Squadron on 11/09/1940 but after only a week it was re-allocated to 99 Squadron based at Newmarket. This was on 18/09/1940 and on 25/09/1940, T2546 flew its first operational mission, it having carried out no operational flying with 9 Squadron. Three crews seemed to have shared use of the aircraft in the four week period leading up to the raid on Berlin. (See Appendix III for operational details of aircraft and crew).

The aircraft took off from Newmarket airfield and headed out over the North Sea towards Berlin. The weather was already deteriorating and the crew consisting of Captain, Acting F/Lt K.T.A. Harvey together with 2nd Pilot Sgt D.C. W. Fortier, Navigator, P/O W.T.A Womack, Wireless Operator/Air Gunner Sgts R.T. Peach and L.S.Hill and Rear Gunner P/O E.S.I. Hallows would have been feeling a little apprehensive about making such a long flight as a prelude to an attack on the German capital in such conditions. Although they had flown in T2546 on one

39

previous occasion their regular aircraft was T2739, VF-V. In fact, records show that this latter aircraft was allocated to them on the night of 29/10/1940 and it is probable that this aircraft became unserviceable just prior to take off, necessitating a transfer to VF-A. Some reports also show the Rear-Gunner to have been a Sgt Parker rather than P/O Hallows but all post-operation reports record this position as having been filled by P/O Hallows.

Little mention is made of the success or not of the mission that night but it would seem that all of 99 Squadron's aircraft reached the target area. They now embarked on the return journey. At some point during the mission T2546's radio equipment failed. Because of the low cloud and poor visibility navigation had been by Dead-Reckoning for almost the entire flight but as the radio had failed there was no way the crew could cross check their position by D/F. Under such conditions of low visibility Dead Reckoning could become a very chancy method of determining an aircraft's position and by midnight VF—A must have become totally lost. Under these circumstances it is likely that the captain, F/Lt Harvey, made the decision to make a slow descent through the cloud in order to get a visual observation of the ground. Unfortunately he chose to do this in an area where Northumberland's moorland reached up into the very same cloud and the aircraft crashed on Blakehope Fell, about a mile west of the Junction of what are now the A 68 and A696 trunk roads at a Elishaw, and approximately three miles north west of Otterburn Village. The RAF describe the crash as being at Bagraw and indeed there is a farm of that name near this point. The actual crash site was just to the south of the summit of Blakehope Fell and as it crashed VF—A smashed through the stone wall which was the boundary between Blakehope and Dargues Hope Farms. As a result of the crash the Rear Gunner was killed and as the squadron records note P/O Hallows to have been killed that night it would seem to be fairly certain that it was P/0 Hallows who was the unfortunate occupant of that position.

Although the aircraft caught fire, a common occurrence with Wellington crashes, the remainder of the crew escaped with their lives with just one receiving minor injuries. The fire became quite fierce and rounds of machine gun ammunition began to explode and as some of these were tracer bullets it developed into an impromptu pyrotechnic display, which is still recalled by some local people to this day. This same local memory recalls that the surviving crew made their way down from the crashed aircraft and went to the "Redesdale Arms" public house known locally as the "First and Last".

There is no record of what happened to the crew after that, either in official records, or from local memories, but it would be safe to assume that they were collected by RAF transport and returned to their base at Newmarket.

The sergeant who was in charge of the airmen responsible for the removal of the remains of the aircraft was billeted with the Farrell family at Brownrigg Cottages, and Mrs Farrell received 1s 9d (about 9 p.) per day from the RAF for his board and lodging. Although the aircraft had caught fire it had remained remarkably intact. It was brought down to the main road (A 68) in large sections (fuselage and wings) using horses and equipment belongings to James Thornton of Blakehope Farm. Once at the roadside these sections were then removed using the standard RAF Queen Mary transporter.

Junkers Ju88 VB+KM   Werke Nr 7122   28/05/1942

Arguably the Ju88 was probably the best and most useful aircraft of the Luftwaffe throughout the war. It served as night fighter, medium bomber, ground attack aircraft and in many other roles including photo-reconnaissance. Rather like the British Mosquito it was the forerunner of today's MRCA.

Its designers, A. Gass and W. Ewer had spent some time in the USA studying the innovative techniques of stressed metal skin construction and were so impressed by this method that they decided to utilise it when designing the new aircraft in 1935. It was to be a fast, medium, unarmed bomber. The prototype first flew in December 1936 and the type began to enter limited operational service just as the war started in September 1939. It became available in large numbers just before the Battle of Britain commenced in 1940. It was soon recognised by high ranking Luftwaffe officers that it was a very competent aircraft and capable of easy adaptation. It was not very long before fighter, photo-reconnaissance and other versions were developed and entered service. It served in every theatre of war that the Luftwaffe was involved in.

A new crew commanded by Lt. Fritz Gortam had arrived at Orly airfield on 15/03/1941. The crew had formed at Fritzlar only shortly before and been posted to 2. Staffel of Aufklärangsgruppe Ob.d.L (Obersbefehlshaber der Luffwaffe), a photo reconnaissance unit. On 26/05/1941 Ju88A-1 Werk Nr 7122 coded VB+KM was flown from Orly to the airfield of Lanveoc-Poulnic, near Brest in readiness for an operational flight to Glasgow in order to photograph the damage caused by previous air raids. The pilot, Herbert Niepel, had only flown 4 operational missions previously whilst the W/Op, Gfr. Joseph Lindorfer had flown 6. In addition to these two members of the crew and the commander, Lt Gortam, a fourth member of the crew, Gfr Heinrich Matthius, described as a mechanic, was to be on board the aircraft. The flight was planned to take place on 27/05/1941 but was cancelled on that day due to bad weather. However the weather cleared on the next day, 28/05 and at 10:00 the aircraft took off on its mission to Glasgow. The aircraft flew towards Scotland by transiting the Republic of Ireland, a route taken by many German aircraft flying missions from France to Scotland. This was a relatively trouble free course for these aircraft as although the Republic of Ireland was neutral, the right to intercept and intern these aircraft was never exercised probably because the Irish authorities did not have the equipment necessary to carry that out.

On the same day , 43 Squadron based at Drem flew 12 of its Hurricanes to Prestwick in Ayrshire. This was one of Fighter Commands "crack" squadrons and the purpose of their temporary transfer to Prestwick was to provide air protection for the British Home Fleet which was returning through the Western Approaches after operations which culminated in the sinking of the German battleship "Bismark".

No sooner had the squadron landed at Preswick than a single enemy aircraft was reported just to the south of Glasgow. At 13:50 two of 43 Squadrons' Hurricanes were immediately "scrambled". Their mission would be to intercept and destroy this intruder. F/Lt du Vivier, a Belgian, flying Hurricane Z3031, and F/O Gzajkowski, a Pole, flying Hurricane Z3079 spotted the aircraft, a Ju88, flying due east at 24,000 feet just to the south east of Glasgow. They gave chase but unfortunately just as they were about to overhaul their quarry F/O Gzajkowski's aircraft developed a serious oil leak and he had to turn away and make a forced landing at an airfield still in the process of being built. The identity of this airfield is not recorded but Crosby-on-Eden, Charter Hall, and Milfield were all being built but not yet complete at around that time. F/Lt du Vivier, however, persisted with his chase and finally opened fire on the Ju88. He raked the enemy aircraft with several bursts of fire and eventually pieces began to break away from it. F/Lt du Vivier's own aircraft was either hit by debris from the damaged Ju88 or perhaps by return fire, and the aircraft began to loose oil rapidly. He therefore broke off the engagement and landed at Acklington. The aircraft he had attacked was VB+KM.

The Ju88 was first seen by witnesses on the ground at 14:15, when it was obvious that it was being attacked and was in difficulty. Pieces were seen to fall from the aircraft and eventually it crashed 1½ miles south east of Kirndean Farm on Boghall Hill. This is itself about 4 ½ miles north east of Newcastleton. Pieces of wreckage were subsequently found at Florida, about 1 mile to the west of Kirndean Farm and also at Foulshiels a further 3 miles to the west. From the line of these pieces of wreckage and the final crash site of the aircraft it would appear that it was most likely that the aircraft was flying on a course just slightly south of due east.

Walter Elliot, whose father farmed Kirndean, together with the Kirndean shepherd, Jock Knox, made their way to the crash site as quickly as possible. Once there they found that two of the crew, Lt Gortam and Gfr Matthius, were already dead but that Herbert Niepel, the pilot and Joseph Lindorfer, the W/Op were alive and well. They took them into custody with the aid of their pitchforks and escorted them back down to Kirndean Farm. Mr Jasper Dodds of Riccarton Farm, which was a little further up Liddesdale appeared with his car, and was persuaded to take the two airmen into the police station in Newcastleton. They were then transferred to Jedburgh Police Station.

From there they must have been taken to a RAF establishment as there are a considerable amount of intelligence records regarding their interrogation by RAF personnel. The capture of this part crew was significant in that they were the first Luftwaffe airmen to be taken prisoner who had completed their training wholly within the period since the start of hostilities. Therefore any information gleaned from them gave RAF intelligence a fair insight into how the pressure of war was affecting the Luftwaffe's training programmes. A fact brought to light by this interrogation was that it seems most likely that Lt Gortam and Gfr. Matthius died as result of the attacks on their aircraft by the RAF fighter aircraft and not as a result of the subsequent crash.

In addition to the crew being interrogated the wreckage of the Ju88 was also minutely analysed. It was found to have been struck by at least 39 rounds of the Hurricane's .303 ammunition. Three MG 15 machine guns (the standard Luftwaffe defensive armament) were recovered from the wreckage. It was thought that the aircraft had been built in the late autumn of 1940, as maker's identification plates revealed that the aircraft's two Junkers Jumo 211 inverted V-12 engines had been built by Junkers Flug Motor Zweigwerk at Magdeberg in October 1940.

This wreckage was removed from the crash site within days. A team of horses belonging to Mr. Little of Dinlabyre Farm was used to drag the aircraft's engines down to Kirndean Farm where they were loaded on to a Queen Mary trailer. It is very likely that the remainder of the wreckage was also removed in this way.

F/Lt du Vivier was subsequently awarded the Belgium Croix du Guerre on 21/07/1944, in respect of this and another action. In August 1941 he took temporary command of the Squadron when Squadron Leader T. D. Morgan was forced to relinquish command when he was hospitalised after ditching in the sea just off North Berwick. S/L Morgan had been attacking an enemy aircraft at the time.

Miles Master III W8594   29/09/1941

The Miles   Master was an advanced training aircraft. Its' intended use was for preparing newly qualified pilots for their eventual training in single engined fighters. To this end an aircraft had to be more powerful and manoeuvrable than an elementary trainer yet docile enough to be forgiving in inexperienced hands. The Master was ideally suited to this role.

The innovative and very original Miles design team produced the Kestrel aircraft as a private venture in 1937. The Air Ministry were impressed by this aircraft and decided that it was the answer to a need which they had been trying to satisfy, without much success, for the previous 18 months. It was decided that a modified version of the aircraft more than met specification T6/36. This aircraft was powered by a Rolls-Royce Kestrel V-12 of 715h.p. and its initial order as the Master I, was the largest single order for a trainer in RAF history. However, the Kestrel engine was already being phased out of production as other types of aircraft it powered became obsolescent and a new version of the Master, the Mark II, powered by a Bristol Mercury 9 cylinder radial engine of 870 h.p. was planned. Unfortunately the Master II then became one of the first aircraft to suffer from the Air Ministry's nervousness about the continuity of supply of British aircraft engines. In the case of the Master this meant a delay of a year in production while an alternative American engine, the Pratt and Whitney Wasp Junior, was being chosen and then delivered in sufficient quantities, since production of both British and American powered aircraft was to be a parallel operation. The Pratt and Whitney Twin Wasp Junior was a 14 cylinder two row radial engine of 820h.p. and the aircraft powered by it was designated Master III. The Master I entered service in 1939, followed by the Mk II and Mk III in early 1940. The Master was a low wing monoplane mainly of wooden construction and was built by Phillips and Powis. It was a two seat aircraft with the instructor behind the pupil in a seat capable of being raised so that the instructor had a good view of landing etc. Production aircraft were covered by specification 16/38 and eventually 900 MkI's, 1717 Mk II's and 602 Mk III's were built. All three types of Master gained the respect of the pilots who were fortunate enough to fly them and they were described as a "delight to fly".

Master III, W8594, started its RAF career with 59 OTU at RAF

View of Tarn Beck as seen from the area of the crash site of Master W8549

Crosby-on-Eden on 27/08/1941.It was to prove a very short career indeed. Only a month later early in the afternoon of Friday, 29/09/1941, Master W8594 took off with Sgt. G. F. Hillier, a New Zealander, at the controls. He was due to take part in an air to air camera gun exercise. Sgt. Hillier had started his flying at 1EFTS in New Zealand and at some time been sent to Canada to complete his flying training, probably under the auspices of the BCATP. Whilst in Canada he was stationed with 66 SFTS at Dunnville, Ontario. He was awarded his wings on 03/07/1941 and was probably shipped to Britain immediately after that. The task of 59 OTU was to train newly qualified pilots to fly Hawker Hurricanes operationally. No.8 course comprising 20 Canadian, 19 New Zealand, 1 Belgian, 1 American and 3 Australian airmen commenced on 09/09/1941 and Sgt Hillier was among those 19 New Zealanders. To assist in the transition between relatively low powered, slow elementary trainers and the very high powered, fast Hurricane the unit had a few Masters on its strength and it was in these that the novice fighter pilots spent their first few hours of training. Sgt Hillier had a total of 185 hours of flying at this time of which 106 hours were solo. Of this total 8 hours had been spent flying Master of which 5 were solo.

The area surrounding the meeting point of the Cumberland/Northumberland boundary and the Anglo-Scottish Border is

Confluence of Tarn Beck and Gair Burn, just to the South of the crash site of Master W8549.

of a very remote and stark nature. About 6 miles due south of the Border the Northumberland /Cumberland boundary is formed by a small stream known as the Gair Burn.. About 2 to 3 miles to the south east of the point where it rises the Gair burn is joined by the Tarn Beck, which itself rises about 3 miles to the west of the point of confluence. From then on the combined waters form the River Irthing which meanders off in a generally south easterly direction. After about 1½ miles there are two farm steadings which straddle the river, Red Sike being to the west , and Paddaburn to the east. The river continues to be the county boundary.

In the mid afternoon of Friday, 29/09/1941, teenager William Selby together with his uncle, John Robson were setting out from Red Sike to travel to Haltwhistle for the Draft Ewe Sale the next day. The ewes had already been taken to Haltwhistle earlier in the day and William and his uncle were due to stay overnight there in order to attend the sale the next day. They would have to travel about 3 miles to Chirnsike Lodge before they reached the tarmac road which would take them to Gilsland. As they passed Paddaburn they met Joe Telford who was cleaning sheep drains next to the track. All of them heard an aircraft diving and then when they turned round to look saw smoke rising from the low hill which formed a spur between the Gair Burn and the Tarn Beck. Joe Telford immediately headed off in the direction of the crash whilst William and his uncle continued on their journey. William made a slight detour to call in at the farm at Lampert where he knew there was a telephone and from there contacted the police to alert them of the crash. In the meantime Joe Telford had reached the crashed aircraft, which had been on fire and was just to the east of Archie's Pike, a small, slightly round topped hill in an otherwise featureless landscape. He soon assessed that there was nothing that could be done to help the pilot of the aircraft and he returned to Paddaburn to await the arrival of the authorities.

Little is known of the subsequent removal of Sgt Hillier's body, for it was the Master which he was piloting that had crashed on that very remote small hill, and neither is there any recollection of the aircraft being recovered. However, it must have been recovered as W8594's record's show that between 29/09/1941 and 12/10/1941 it was "Presumed Struck-off"(PS0) but on 12/10/1941 was officially "Struck-off Charge" (SOC) indicating that it was probably lying at an undisclosed RAF establishment waiting to be assessed.

Although the purpose of the tragic flight that day is recorded as an "Air to Air Camera Gun exercise" it is probable that Sgt Hillier's aircraft was being used as the target aircraft as the Masters were not equipped with weapons of any kind (and therefore no weapons bay to accommodate the camera gun). It is therefore likely that another purpose of the flight was to increase his experience of flying the Master.

The accident report surmises that the aircraft became lost in a sudden heavy rainstorm. Sgt. Hillier then reduced altitude to try and locate his position and struck the hill which was obscured from his view by cloud and mist. Sadly he never gained the further experienced he required. Local recall tells that he was one of three New Zealand airmen who all signed up for the RNZAF at the same time and who all came to 59 OTU at the same time. Tragically, the story goes, all three lost their lives before their training was completed; all within a short space of time and all in crashes in the Northumberland/Cumberland/Border area. There is no official confirmation of this story although there is likely to be an element of truth in it as several other New Zealand airmen did lose their lives whilst serving with 59 OTU.

Hawker Hurricane II Z2349   13/10/1941

A significant proportion of flights undertaken by military aircraft in World War II were not combat, operational or training sorties but were ferry flights. These ferry flights took place for a number of reasons including delivery of new aircraft from factories , returning repaired aircraft to their units, transfer of aircraft between units etc. etc. For many of these flights British aircraft were piloted by personnel of the Air Transport Auxiliary (ATA). This was an organisation set up by the government at the start of hostilities specifically for the purpose of aircraft delivery. It recruited personnel who already had a pilots licence but for one reason or another (gender or age) were considered unsuitable for combat. The RAF also had its own internal organisation for dealing with these aircraft movements and had dedicated Delivery Flights and Ferry Units.

Hawker Hurricane II Z2349 was being ferried to RAF Turnhouse on 13/10/1941. The aircraft, as described in the Background section of this guide, was taken on charge by the RAF at 19 MU on 23/09/1940. It remained there until 28/12/1940 when it was issued to 6SFTS. This long period of not being utilised, which started during the Battle of Britain emphasises the fact that replacement aircraft were never a limiting factor during that critical campaign, the crucial possible shortfall being that of replacement aircrew. 6SFTS must have had little need of the aircraft and it was returned to 19 MU on 11/01/1941. Later that month on 30/01/1941 the aircraft was once again issued, this time to 249 Squadron based at RAF North Weald. As noted in the "Backgrounds" section it was a pilot from this Squadron, F/L J.B.Nicolson, who gained Fighter Commands only Victoria Cross on 16/08/1940. Records of the aircraft then show Z2349 to have been transferred away from this squadron on 27/04/1941. At about this time 249 Squadron would no longer have had a use for the aircraft as they were embarked on the aircraft carriers H.M.S. Ark Royal and H.M.S. Furious in order that they could fly brand new Hurricanes from these aircraft carriers in to the beleaguered island of Malta.

After this transfer 71(Eagle) Squadron became the next user of the aircraft. This Squadron had acquired its name because the majority of its pilots were Americans who had volunteered to fly in the RAF to help the British cause before the USA declared war against Germany and Japan. Having flown Hurricanes Is for some time 71 Squadron started to convert to Hurricane IIs in April 1941 but it is not clear whether Z2349 went to them at Martlesham Heath or whether the Squadron acquired the aircraft when it moved to the North Weald in June 1941, it having perhaps being left there by 249 Squadron when it departed. There is scant evidence that Z2349 ever flew operationally with 71 Squadron and by June 1941 this Squadron was converting to Spitfires.

Once again the aircraft became surplus to requirements and on 13/06/1941 it was transferred to 247 Squadron based at RAF Predannack in Cornwall. Sgt Deuntzer, thought to be South African, ferried Z2349 to Predannack on 17/06/1941 and it was he who flew it on most of its operational flights with that Squadron. Its last known flight with 247 Squadron was on 10/09/1941, that Squadron being converted to Hurricane IIc at around that time. The official record of the movements of the aircraft (Air Ministry Form 78) then shows it to have been taken on charge by 310

Squadron on 20/09/1941. But no record of it can be found as ever having operated with 310 Squadron. That squadron was based at RAF Montrose and it is probable that Z2349 was being delivered to them there. Certainly other Hurricanes from the same batch flew with 310 Squadron whilst based at Montrose.

The police report on the crash which eventually took place on 13/10/1941 describes the aircraft as being on a flight from Anglesey to Turnhouse. It's pilot that day was Sgt. John Manby who had earlier been on the strength of 242 Squadron based at RAF Valley in Anglesey. That Squadron disbanded in early October 1941 aand Sgt. Manby was posted out of the Squadron on 02/10/1941.

At the time of the accident which occurred during this ferry flight to Turnhouse whichever unit was resopnsible for Z2349 was a member of 9 Group of Fighter Command. This fact is recorded in the accident report and is unlikely to be incorrect as it is highly improbable that 9 group would accept the loss of the aircraft unless it was definitely one of their aircraft. The same RAF report on the crash records the aircraft's operating unit as 3 Delivery Flight. No operating records of this unit can be found. As already argued it would be unlikely that 9 Group would accept responsibility for the aircraft unless it was being operated by a unit within the command structure of 9 Group. It is assumed, therefore, that 3 Delivery Flight was an internal organisation within 9 Group whose function was the ferrying and delivery of aircraft to units within that group and to and from units outside that group. But neither 247 nor 310 Squadron was part of 9 Group, so why was Z2349 in Anglesey and where had it been since 10/09/1941. Interestingly, and intriguingly, 242 Squadron which Sgt Manby had served in up to 02/10/1941,had been part of 9 Group up until the time it was disbanded.

It is probable that Z2349 was being flown from Predannack to Montrose in stages as it certainly would not have had the operational range to enable it to carry out a flight of that distance in one step. Perhaps it had arrived in Anglesey some time before its final flight and had lingered there until somebody became available to fly it on its onward journey. That somebody took the form of Sgt Manby. This is conjecture, the only certain fact being that between 10/09/1941 and the 13/10/1941 no accurate record of the whereabouts of Z2349 seems to exist.

On the day of its ferry flight to Turnhouse, which is just to the west of Edinburgh, Z2349 was seen flying below the low cloud approximately 1½ miles south of Riccarton Junction. The time was at 12.15pm. The aircraft did not, however, arrive at Turnhouse and it was posted as missing along with its pilot, Sgt John Manby. Riccarton Junction was, and is, a very remote place indeed. It was where the Border Counties

49

**Phaupknowe, (now spelt Fawhope Knowe). The area of the site of
the crash of Hurricane Z2349 is on the high ground shrouded in
mist beyond the trees - just to the left of centre of photograph.**

railway, which followed the River North Tyne northwards from Hexham
joined the main railway line from Carlisle to Edinburgh, known as the
Waverly Route. So remote was Riccarton Junction that all the supplies for
its small close knit community were brought in by rail and there was a
small Co-op store on the platform. Most of the inhabitants were railway
employees but James Beattie was the shepherd at Fawhope Knowe Farm.
This farm was named after the hill immediately to the north-east of the
single track Border Counties Railway. On the morning of 14/09/1941
James Beattie set off on his usual route to "look" all the ewes on the hill. At
around 9.30 am he had reached a point overlooking the railway at a place
where it ran on a high embankment known as Palmer's Bank. He noticed
Walter Rutherford, the shepherd at Saughtree Farm coming along the
hillside on that farm's part of the fell. The two met up and as they did so the
wreckage of an aircraft came into view. On reaching the wreckage they
found the pilot's body. They came to the conclusion that he had died
instantly at the time of the crash, and there was little more that could be
achieved by staying at the crash site. James Beatie returned to Riccarton
Junction from where the authorities were informed probably by the one
public phone which existed at "the Junction" and was situated in the
station buildings.

Sgt Manby's body was brought down from the hill and taken to

50

the local policeman's house at Riccarton. This was done using a horse and cart, firstly following the Fawhope Knowe Sike down, then crossing the Border Counties Line at Palmers Bank, and finally returning to follow the burn to reach Riccarton. The body was then taken to RAF Crosby-on-Eden.

RAF personnel arrived to guard the wreckage and were billeted at Riccarton Farm. After only a short period of time the wreckage was removed from the hillside. This was done utilising the large sledges used to take fodder out to the hill ewes during winter storms. The wreckage was brought down to Riccarton Junction where it was loaded onto a railway flatbed wagon, for an onward journey to a destination neither recorded or remembered. This mode of removal does, however, probably confer on this incident a uniqueness, in that it is probably the only wreckage recovered from high ground by rail.

After the wreckage had gone, and the RAF guard along with it, some of the local children including James Beattie's daughter, Mary, went up to the crash site. Mary remembers that the perspex was easily cut and that the children spent some time making trinkets from the salvaged pieces. It seems very likely that some of these survive to this day, the only physical reminder of that sad day.

The accident report by the RAF surmises that Sgt Manby probably left turning back until it was too late when he found himself in a "mountainous area" (RAF description) in conditions of low cloud and poor visibility. He had 195 hours of flying of which 120 had been spent flying Hurricanes; not a lot of experience by modern standards, and not enough to outwit the treachery of the Border Hills and their attendant weather.

Note:- Fawhope Knowe is a modern spelling. On old maps and in archive records the spelling is Phaupknowe.

Hawker Hurricane II Z3150   03/11/1941

43 Squadron was stationed in the Border area several times during the early stages of the war. In October 1941 it was transferred to RAF Acklington for what was to prove to be a stay, for both Squadron and Station, of unprecedented length. The Squadron left in May 1942.

When Z3150 was delivered to 43 Squadron on 19/04/41 the Squadron was based at Drem, in the Lothian area. The aircraft had been allotted to 46 MU on 02/03/1941 but had not been delivered to that unit until 03/04/1941. The following day the aircraft was transferred to 27 MU where it stayed until issued to 43 Squadron.

Not many weeks later, on 04/06/1941 P/O Hukam Chand Mehta was posted in to 43 Squadron. He was Indian and had started his flying training in India with 12 ITS at Begumpet. He subsequently moved to Britain for the remainder of his training progressing through 12 FTS at Grantham and 9 FTS at Hullavington, before receiving his operational training on Hurricanes at 56 OTU stationed at Sutton Bridge in Lincolnshire. He rapidly became a popular and well liked member of the squadron and for a reason which is completely unclear acquired the nickname "Joe".

His operational flying started almost immediately with some local flying in Hurricane Z2407 on 06/06/1941. Like most of the other pilots of 43 Squadron he flew almost everyday and sometimes twice a day. The vast majority of these flights were routine patrols interspersed occasionally with some form of training flight. On 12/06/1941 he flew Hurricane II Z3150 for the first time. This aircraft had by this time been flown by the O/C of 43 Squadron, S/L T. D. Morgan, and during May it was he who was flying it when it was used to shoot down two enemy aircraft during the so called "Clydeside Blitz".

On 03/11/1941 Z3150, coded FT-V took off at 10:35 for an X-plot exercise and was flown by Sgt. Tweedale. During this exercise P/O Mehta few Hurricane II Z2772 and all the aircraft returned at 10:50. Later that day between 14:30 and 14:40, Z3150 once again took off this time flown by P/O Mehta. It was accompanied by three other Hurricanes, Z2639, flown by F/Lt May, Z2667, flown by Sgt Ball and Z2772 flown by Sgt Barclay. The object of this flight was formation practice. At 15:20 all the aircraft except Z3150 returned to Acklington. Almost immediately, at 15:40, F/Lt May took off in Z2639 to search for the missing aircraft. He returned at 17:40 having had no success. The following day 04/11/1941, three aircraft took off to continue to search for P/O Mehta's aircraft. F/Lt May in Z2639 was accompanied by Sgt. Tweedale in Z3336 and Sgt. Williams in Z2772. They left at 09:45 and returned to Acklington at 10:30 once again having had a fruitless search. The Squadron, however, were obviously anxious to know the fate of their comrade-in-arms as they put up another aircraft to search, this time Hurricane Z3265 flown by S/L Morgan. He took off at 14:40 and returned at 15:55. Once again without success.

It seems very likely that by this time the Roxburghshire police already knew that the aircraft had crashed, and where, as their records of events are dated 03/11/1941. They did, however, have some difficulty in identifying the aircraft and this is possibly why the RAF at Acklington were not informed immediately and hence why they, the RAF, were still

The summit of Peel Fell, close to the site of the crash of Hurricane Z3150.

sending out aircraft to carry out searches. It was almost certain that the crash of the aircraft was observed as an almost "spot" time is given for its occurrence. This time was stated to be between 15:45 and 16:00. The police report does not reveal who found the crashed aircraft, but that person was probably also responsible for recording the time of the crash. The site of the crash is stated as being 2 miles north east of the Peel shepherd's house and as this was, and is, an area of very sparse population it would seem likely that it was the Peel shepherd, David Jackson, who saw the aircraft crash. It was certainly he and P.C. Robertson who later found the aircraft. The aircraft was found 300 feet from the summit of Peel Fell and was completely buried except for the tail. P/O Mehta's body was not discovered immediately and some time elapsed before it was finally located. It was found ten feet from the wreckage and buried eight feet deep. This gives some idea of the force of the impact when Z3150 hit the fell-side. The police account of the discovery of the body is extremely graphic and detailed and makes very harrowing reading indeed.

The cause of the crash is stated as being an Error of Judgement by P/O Mehta. He had been the leader of the formation training flight and after receiving a homing wireless message led one of the less experienced pilots into cloud whilst following the course provided by the message. The under training pilot became separated from P/O Mehta and presumed that he, P/O Mehta that is, had climbed to get above cloud and did likewise. P/O/ Mehta had however descended whilst in the cloud with the tragic end result detailed above. It was further concluded that if better use had been made of the radio aids at Sector HQ, the accident could have been avoided. "Joe" Mehta had completed 284 hours of flying at the time of the accident of which 184 hours had been spent flying Hurricanes and was therefore not an inexperienced pilot.

The wreckage of Z3150 was recovered by No. 12 Mobile Section, 63 MU, RAF Carluke. However, as will be seen later in this guide, not every last piece of wreckage was removed.

P/O Hukam Chand Mehta was cremated at the West Road Crematorium, Newcastle-upon-Tyne. The ceremony, carried out according to Hindu tradition, was conducted by Mr. N.K.Roy and was attended by a representative of the High Commissioner for India.

Hawker Hurricane I   N2428   12/06/1942

By June 1942 very few day fighter squadrons involved in the air defence of the UK were still operating Hurricanes. Any Mark I Hurricanes still in service were mostly at OTU's and even the Mark IIs were allocated to squadrons based in areas of low threat. The Hurricane IIB was, however, making a name for its self as a fighter-bomber, in which role it earned itself the nickname "Hurribomber". And in overseas theatres the Hurricane was still being used as a front line fighter. This meant that there was still a pressing need for OTUs to be training Hurricane pilots.

59 OTU, still based at RAF Crosby-on- Eden had acquired N2428 on 31/07/1942. It had come to that unit after having served with two front line squadrons and two other OTUs. In fact it was built to contract number 751458/38 by Hawkers as was N2522 another Hurricane I which crashed in the Cheviot Hills on 24/04/1941. The similarity did not end there however, both aircraft being delivered to the RAF on the same day, 26/10/1939, and then after both had been held at different MUs being issued to the same squadron, 56 based at North Weald, within days of each other. The service career of N2428 then diverged slightly from that of its stablemate, serving with 5 OTU and 308 Squadron during the late summer and early autumn of 1940. However, on 14/11/1940 N2428 rejoined its previous companion by being issued to 55 OTU at RAF Ouston. It remained there, outliving its contemporary,N2522, until transferred to 22 MU on 11/10/1941. It was then issued to 59 OTU. On 28/02/1942 it was involved in an accident of some kind which resulted in some damage. It's repairs at Crosby-on-Eden commenced on 10/03/1942 and it was returned

to the flight line on 28/03/1942

Like its contemporary N2428 also came to an ignominious end. In the early afternoon of 12/06/1942 the aircraft was taking part in a formation practice flown by Sgt Donald Fraser, a New Zealander. Sgt Fraser was a member of the No. 18 course with 59 OTU. At about 13:50 the formation leader, an instructor, led the formation into an area of cloud. Sgt. Fraser became lost and disorientated . Due to his inexperience (he had a total of 121 hours flying with only 27 of those being on Hurricanes) he probably descended to try and establish his position. Unfortunately he chose to do this at a point where some high ground known as Limekiln Edge, was shrouded by the same cloud in which he was flying. The aircraft struck the ground and burst into flames. Unfortunately Sgt Fraser was killed instantly. The crash had occurred about 300 yards yards north east of Whitrope Cottages. These cottages overlook the southern portal of Whitrope Tunnel on the Waverly Route railway line between Carlisle and Edinburgh and stand beside the Hawick to Newcastleton road(B6399). The crash site was about 300-400 metres to the south east of this road.

One of the occupants of the cottages was a Mr. Graham, a railway signalman at Whitrope signal box. His daughter, Catherine, clearly remembers the crash, but also remembers that the few locals who were aware of it were told little of the details of the aircraft or it's pilot. Catherine recalls that the wreckage was removed fairly quickly and that because the road was so close very few problems were encountered. Once the aircraft had been removed Catherine and the other children from the area went up to where the Hurricane had crashed and scoured the ground for fragments of perspex. As noted in the crash of Z2349 these pieces of perspex were much sought after, and long hours were spent "whittling" them into rings and forms of simple trinket.

But New Zealand had lost yet another of its sons in the fight against tyranny.

Boeing Fortress IIA   FK204   11/08/1942

This aircraft was one of a batch of 45 such aircraft offset to Britain under the terms of the Land-Lease arrangements. Fortress IIA was the RAF designation for the Boeing B-17E and these aircraft were utilised mainly by squadrons of Coastal Command.

The B-17 Flying Fortress was among the most successful aircraft produced by the American aircraft industry during WWII. It was designed by the Boeing Airplane Company as a private venture, in order to fulfil a need which they perceived was likely to arise. When the prototype first flew in July 1935 it was revolutionary both in size and aerodynamic shape. Intended to be a heavy bomber it was powered by four Wright Cyclone GR-1820-39 nine cylinder radial engines. It was slow to enter service, however, and this was due to the undermining of confidence in the aircraft of various Government Departments due to two unfortunate accidents during the development programme. This lack of confidence was exacerbated by the doubt expressed by some senior USAAC officers regarding the concept of strategic air power. Having acquired turborchargers for its Cyclone engines, and thus considerably more power, the first operational version of the type, the B-17A entered service in 1937. This was followed in 1939 by the B-17B whose main new feature was the revolutionary Norden gyroscopic bomb sight which was linked to the flying controls via the auto-pilot equipment. The early versions of the B-17 were armed with five hand held 0.5in. machine guns and it was considered, like the Wellington, that when flying in formation a number of aircraft with this armament would create enough defensive firepower to deter attacking fighters and hence be safe to use in daylight bombing attacks. In May 1941 the RAF took delivery of 20 examples of one of the earlier versions (the B-17C) and designated them Fortress I. It was used by them for daylight bombing raids, but using the aircraft's ability to fly at extremely high altitude as its main defence. However many technical problems arose as a result of these operations and the experience gained by the RAF before the USA entered the war helped to develop later versions of the aircraft which were more competent. In these later versions (B-17E, F & G) a completely redesigned tail fin and rudder was adopted and the aircraft acquired three power operated gun turrets each equipped with two 0.5in. machine guns. In the G version a further turret was added in the nose and the single hand held machine guns were replaced by twin mounted weapons. The total defensive armament was then thirteen 0.5in. machine guns. By the end of World War II the B-17 had made a huge contribution to the USAAF war effort and had completely vindicated Boeing's fortuitous foresight of the requirement for such an aircraft.

FK204, therefore, as a Fortress IIA(B-17E) was one of the later much redesigned aircraft. It was delivered from Boeing's factory at Seattle to United Airlines repair depot at Cheyenne, Wyoming on 18/05/1942. This repair depot had been set up to carry out all the modification work which "on line" development work had shown to be necessary, and which, if they had been carried out on the production line at Seattle would have slowed manufacture of B-17s to an unacceptable level. It was flown to the UK on 19-20/06/1942 and was held by Scottish Aviation until sent to the Burtonwood repair depot on 27/06/1942. All B-17's entering the UK, even those intended for the USAAF, passed through Burtonwood to have further modifications made to them. These modifications, mostly to radio and electrical equipment, were in order that the aircraft were compatible with British air traffic control and IFF systems. This work completed FK204's next port of call was the Royal Aircraft Establishment (RAE) at Farnborough on 01/07/1942. No reason is given for this move but it could well have been for flight tests to establish handling characteristics as this was one of the first B-17E's to arrive in the UK. It is likely that the RAE found further items for modification as the aircraft arrived back at Burtonwood on 11/07/1942. These complete the aircraft was assigned to 220 Squadron at RAF Nutts Corner in Northern Island on 25/07/1942.

However, on the same day, the aircraft now coded NR-N, was transferred to the airfield at Ballykelly, also in Northern Ireland. At that time 220 Squadron was using both of these airfields and had only just converted to Fortresses. They were being used for anti-submarine (A/S) patrols whilst escorting convoys.

And it was for this purpose that NR-N took off from Ballykelly on 10/08/1942. Take off time was 1427 and the crew consisted of Captain (1st Pilot) W/C. R.T.F Gates, 2nd Pilot P/O K.L.H. Ramsden plus Sgt A.T. Hill, Sgt H. Tasche, Sgt E. Thornton, Sgt J.W. Wood, Sgt W.L. Kean and Cpl R.A. Morrison all of whose duties in the aircraft are unknown. The aircraft's task was to escort convoy SC94 by performing an A/S patrol around it, the largest threat to convoys at that time being German submarines (U-boats). It had aready been established that the mere presence of an aircraft above a convoy was usually enough to keep them at bay, the U-boats having no realistic defence against a determined aircraft attack.

SC94 was an eastbound Atlantic convoy which had set out from Sydney, Cape Breton on 31/07/1942. The convoy consisted of 30 Merchant ships with an escort of 6 warships initially, including the frigates HMCS Assiniboine and HMS Dianthus. On 03/08/1942 the convoy was joined by a further 3 merchant ships and their escort, HMCS Battleford, which had started their voyage from St John's, Newfoundland. Air cover was provide by Catalina flying boats of 73 Squadron of the USAAC. Losses of allied shipping due to attacks by U-boats had been falling for some months but convoy SC94 was to dramatically reverse that trend and become a running battle across mid Atlantic.

First blood was drawn by the U-boats when the SS Spar was torpedoed and sank on 05/08/1942. The covering aircraft detected U-boats but only a few attacks on them were made, and with no success. Revenge was had, however, on 06/08/1942 when HMCS Assiniboine sunk U-210 by a depth charge attack following a hunt which lasted several hours. Advantage swung back to the U-boats on 08/08/1942 when they sank five merchant ships very rapidly, including the ship of the convoy's commodore, the SS Trehata. Commodore Moir was one of the crew who was not rescued. By this daring attack, however, the U-boats revealed their position and the escorts seized on the opportunity immediately. HMS Dianthus detected a U-boat in mid-afternoon. The frigate chased the U-boat around the ocean harrying it with depth charges until in the early evening it submitted and surfaced. Now short of ammunition the commanding officer of HMS Dianthus decided ramming was the only means of sinking the U-boat left to him. At 2230 she charged the U-boat hitting it just forward of the conning tower. The crew of U-379, immediately began to abandon their vessel and not long afterwards it sank stern first into the Atlantic. HMS Nasturtium, one of the famous "Flower Class" corvettes, also detected and attacked a U-boat around this time and claims were made that the submarine was sunk although this was never substantiated.

The following day, 09/08/1942, air cover was provided for the first time by the RAF. Liberator "H" of 120 Squadron, also based at Ballykelly, was first over the convoy and during the next 24 hours was relieved by aircraft "O", "S", "V", "W", and "X" of the same squadron.

The presence of aircraft was not preventing activity of the U-boats and on 10/08/1942 a further 4 merchant ships were torpedoed and sunk. Therefore FK204's arrival over the convoy may have been critical. Unfortunately, neither the convoy records nor squadron records confirm that NR-N ever made contact with the convoy. After Liberator "A" of 120 Squadron had left the convoy the next aircraft reported as arriving for escort duty was Fortress II NR-B of 220 Squadron. This aircraft did not contact the convoy until 05:12 hours on 12/08/1942 almost 36 hours after NR-N should have been there.

The mission although apparently not successfully accomplished was over and, NR-N turned for home. In the meantime the weather at Ballykelly had deteriorated and instructions were received by the aircraft that they should proceed to, and land at Prestwick. However, this airfield was also enveloped in the poor weather making it impossible for NR-N to land there. The aircraft was then in dire need of navigational assistance and this could have been obtained by radio; but for two factors. Firstly there was heavy static on all radio transmissions that night and secondly was the fact that the aircraft's trailing radio aerial could not be wound out when needed as the winch had jammed. Because of the low and widespread cloud the crew were prevented from making any observation of the ground to establish their location, and to all intents the aircraft was lost. Fuel was starting to get low and with no prospect of finding an airfield it was decided to abandon the aircraft. This was around 01:15 and the aircraft was over Greenlaw, just to the north of Coldstream. The whole crew left the aircraft by parachute and all landed safely, six reporting to Kelso police station and two being found near Wooler. When the aircraft was abandoned there must have been very little fuel remaining because at 01:35 the aircraft crashed on Doddington Hill just to the north-east of Wooler. The location of the crash was stated as being 900 yards to the south-east of Doddington Quarry with a trail of debris 600 yards long and 100 to 150 yards wide. This description of the crash site puts it quite close to the tee for the 7th hole of the present day Wooler Golf Club.

An indication of how poor the weather in Northern Ireland had been during those few days was the fact that the two aircraft preceding FK204 on patrol both landed at airfields away from the area after completing their patrols. Liberator "F" of 120 Squadron landed at Silloth whilst Liberator "A" of the same Squadron landed at Charterhall.

Although all the crew of FK204 had survived 11/08/1942 was a day when events had not gone well for 220 Squadron. In addition to the total destruction of FK204, another of the Squadron's aircraft, Fortress IIA NR-J (serial number not known), on returning from escort duty to convoy ONS120 had crashed on landing at Nutts Corner, detonating its full load of depth charges. Once again the aircraft was totally destroyed but this time, sadly, none of the crew survived.

The loss of these two aircraft on the same day would have been very disappointing for the RAF as only eleven Fortress IIAs were operational at this time.

The problem of the trailing aerial and winch remained to dog the B-17E for some time, even among those aircraft serving with the USAAC. The problem was eventually solved by running a permanent wire from a mast just to the rear of the cockpit area, to the tip of the fin and thence to a point midway along the left wing.

FK204 had originally been released from Cheyenne into USAAC service and as such received a USAAC serial number. This was most likely to have been 41-9198. The other Fortress IIA lost by 220 Squadron on 11/08/1942 (NR-J) was most likely to have had USAAC number 41-9201 originally, although there is a small possibility that these two numbers could be transposed.

FK204 had completed 47 hours and 45 minutes of flying time when it came to rest near the 7th tee.

Supermarine Spitfire I R7202 03/02/1943

Probably the most famous of all wartime British aircraft the Spitfire somehow seemed to represent the spirit and hopes of the British nation. It was designed in response to Air Ministry specification F7/30 by Reginald Mitchell who drew on his experience designing the Schneider Trophy winning seaplanes the S5, S6 and S6B when starting work on the new project. The prototype first flew on the 5th March 1936 and was an immediate success. It was powered by the same Rolls - Royce Merlin V -12 engine which was also installed in the Hawker Hurricane prototype. It was, and is , a beautifully proportioned aircraft with almost 100% curved surfaces. This later point became a difficulty when placing the aircraft into mass production, new techniques having to be evolved to manufacture these curved panels. These difficulties were all overcome and the aircraft entered squadron service in Mk I form in July 1938. A new Air Ministry specification, F37/34, was drawn up to cover production versions of the Spitfire.

Subsequently many Marks of the Spitfire were produced most of them consisting of the fitting of an improved version of the Merlin engine. Some later marks were fitted with the larger and much more powerful Rolls - Royce Griffon V - 12 engine. Although a superb aircraft in most respects it was not without some minor faults which could catch out the novice pilot. The narrow track undercarriage and the very long nose which blocked the pilot's forward view in either the take off or landing phase created difficulties for inexperienced pilots. Throughout its service life the Spitfire suffered from lack of range, this being entirely due to the lack of space for internal fuel storage. In the later Griffon engined versions the natural balance of the aerodynamics of the Spitfire was upset and the aircraft became much more difficult to handle.

This particular Spitfire, R7202, a Mark I, was issued to 45MU on 08/03/1941. It was then re-issued to 122 Squadron on 08/05/1941. This squadron was based at RAF Turnhouse at that time. Almost immediately 122 Squadron started to re-equip with the Mk II version of the Spitfire and on 22/06/1941 R7202, being surplus to requirements was transferred to 53 OTU based at RAF Heston, situated on the western fringes of London. In July 53 0TU, together with R7202 moved to RAF Llandow in South Wales. It was whilst based there that on 12/10/1941 R7202 crashed at Wilton Farm suffering Category E damage. This would normally have resulted in the aircraft being Struck Off Charge (SOC) and scrapped. However in this case the decision to SOC was not taken until 15/12/1941 and then when it was, it was immediately rescinded and the aircraft reinstated for use. The repairs to the aircraft must have been very extensive for it was not until 27/06/1942 that it was issued to 57 OTU based at Hawarden in North Wales. RAF Eshott became the base for 57 OTU in November 1942 and it was from that airfield that R7202 made its final flight on 03/02/1943.

There are few details known about this final flight. The aircraft was being flown by Sgt H. R. E. Moureaux of the Free French Air Force and had taken off at 08:40 hours on a routine training flight. It failed to return , and was not seen again until 08/02/1943. The wreckage was found on Darden Rigg by Willy Milburn, the shepherd at Midgy Ha. Sgt Moureaux's body was also found in the wreckage. Darden Rigg is the long flat topped hill at the western end of the Simonside Hills which can be seen to the south of the Rothbury to Otterburn road in the Hepple area.

The official report into the accident records that there seems to have been no mechanical defects with the aircraft and that the aircraft flew into the hillside at high speed and in a horizontal attitude. As the visibility was good and the aircraft was not descending it can be assumed that the aircraft was not lost. It is suggested that the pilot may have been carrying out unauthorised low-flying and simulated "ground strafing," misjudged his altitude and then flown into the hill. For this assumption to have been made there must have been evidence from ground based eyewitnesses of the alleged low flying. This evidence would have been recorded on Air Ministry Form 412 which is a report of the findings of a Court of Inquiry. Unfortunately few of these forms have survived, and this is the reason why the existence of eye-witness evidence can only be conjecture. Although the accident had occurred in clear visibility the reason for the wreckage remaining undiscovered for 5 days was that that almost immediately after the crash a thick fog had descended in the Simonside Hills, making a search almost impossible.

By pure coincidence two other future victims of Border Hills air crashes were also serving with 57 OTU at the time of this accident. Flight Sgt E. L. Brown lost his life when Spitfire, P8587, crashed on the north-eastern side of The Cheviot on 25/03/1943 and P/O J. W. van Hamel was also killed when his Spitfire, NH700, dived into the Simonside Hills in April 1944 only 2 to 3 miles east of the site of the crash of R7202. By this time P/O van Hamel, a Dutchman, was serving with 322 Squadron an operational unit based at RAF Acklington. Both of these stories are told in full in "Where the Hills Meet the Sky".

A crawler tractor was used to remove the bulk of the wreckage from the hill and it is believed that Hepple Whitefield was the base for this operation.

Perhaps this is one of the few crashes in the Border Hills where the hills or the weather or a mechanical defect could not be blamed. It could have just simply been a result of Gallic exuberance.

61

The North American Mustang single engined fighter is an almost perfect example with which to highlight the accelerating rate of technological development of aircraft during the early years of the war.

The Mustang was the result of a request by the British Air Purchasing Commission in April 1940. They had made the request because they considered the Curtis P-40 series of fighters, with which they were being supplied at the time, unsuitable for the aerial combat conditions which had developed in Europe. Because of the seriousness of the war situation and the likelihood of aircraft shortages developing one stipulation of the request was that a prototype would have to be ready in 120 days. North American Aviation bettered this stipulation and rolled out an engineless aircraft in 117 days. Having acquired an engine, an Allison V-1710-39(3FR) liquid cooled V-12, the aircraft first flew in October 1940. From the very start it was apparent that the aircraft was a thoroughbred. So few snags were encountered in the flight test programme that production started almost immediately. The aircraft's fuselage was of the smallest cross-sectional area possible and very clean aerodynamically. The wing, the major technological advance, was of laminar flow design. This was an attempt to get the air to flow around the wing without breaking up into drag inducing eddies. So successful was the aerodynamic shape of the fuselage and the laminar flow wing that the Mustang, although only using an engine of comparable power (1100 h.p.), was nearly 30 m.p.h. faster than the contemporary Mark of the Spitfire. This fine tuning of the aerodynamics of the Mustang also led to another feature being bestowed on it which eventually was the cornerstone of its success. And this was the positioning of the wing slightly further aft than in earlier designs, and once again a spin-off of the more advanced aerodynamics. This in turn allowed a fuel tank to be positioned in the rear fuselage behind the pilot, with an almost doubling of the combat range compared with contemporary fighters. This long range capability was to be a crucial factor in the success of the USAAF's daylight bombing campaign in Europe later in the war as it meant that the bombers could be escorted all the way to their targets. AG617 was among the first Mark I Mustangs to arrive in Britain. Despite all their other good features it was soon found that these original design Mustangs had a distinct weakness. This was their inability to perform at high altitude. This factor was entirely due to the choice of engine which only had a moderate degree of supercharging. The US Defence Department's thinking in the late 1930's was that fighters would be used mostly for coastal defence and ground attack and therefore would not need to have a high altitude capability. As a result the U.S. aero engine industry designed and produced fighter engines only suitable for low altitude.

This shortcoming was soon addressed by the RAF. One of their aircraft was sent to Rolls-Royce who replaced the original Allison engine with one of their own Merlin 66 engines, the type currently being fitted to the Mark IX version of the Spitfire. This engine, with its two speed, two stage supercharger, transformed the higher altitude performance of the Mustang and before long North American were fitting Packard built versions of this engine to Mustangs coming off its' production line.

Arriving in the U.K. by the cargo ship "SS Laurity Swenson" on 19/04/1942, AG617 was sent to a depot at Southport which may have been a facility for the re-assembly of aircraft partially disassembled for shipping purposes. On 11/10/1942 it was transferred to 20 MU where its final modifications, application of roundels etc. etc. would have been carried out. It was then issued to 4 Squadron based at RAF Clifton, near York, on 03/02/1943. This squadron was part of Army Co-operation Command, it having been decided that because of its' poor high altitude performance the Mustang should be utilised for ground attack, and low level photo reconnaissance duties. The aircraft does not seem to have been used until the 10/02/1943 but then appears to have been used on almost a daily basis and sometime more than once a day (see Appendix IV for details), During this time most of 4 Squadron's flying consisted of various types of training but occasionally operational sorties were flown over the Low Countries and Northern France. These operational flights serve to demonstrate the Mustang's long range capability, in that Occupied France could be reached from Northern England.

F/O J. Fisher appears to have been transferred to 4 Squadron in November 1942. He immediately began to undertake training flights in the Squadron's Mustangs but does not seem to have been allocated an individual regular aircraft (see Appendix IV for details).

On the 19/02/1943 F/O Fisher took off from RAF East Moor in Mustang AG617. The take off time was 10:15 and the destination of the flight was to be Edinburgh. The airfield at East Moor, normally the home of bomber squadrons, was used by aircraft of 4 Squadron on a regular basis it being only about 10 minutes flying time from Clifton. On the previous day, 18/02/1943, F/O Fisher had flown AG617 on a tactical reconnaissance exercise from Clifton between 14:29 and16:05,and then flown the aircraft to East Moor at 17:30. He then did some night flying in the same aircraft between 18:30 and 20:15 which completed quite a busy flying day. The purpose of the flight on 19/02 is not known but what is certain is that it was never completed. Thirty eight minutes after takeoff AG617 plunged into the boggy moorland just to the north of Bellingham.

63

It dived into the ground at an angle of 30° and an estimated speed of 350 to 400 mph.

The site of the crash was about two miles north of the road from Otterburn to Bellingham (B6320) and approximately 2 miles west of the main A68 road. To the south of the crash site, on the Bellingham to Otterburn road, was Hareshaw Pit, a busy colliery, with a large number of cottages for its employees.

It was an occupant of one of these cottages, Bobby Armstrong, but known to his friends as "Ginger Bob", who heard the thud of the impact of the Mustang and quickly made his way to the crash site. There would have been little he could have done, for RAF records state that the aircraft's cockpit was 16 feet below the surface of the peat. At first it was not known whether there was a body in the aircraft but eventually F/O Fisher's body was found, and, although the crash had occurred on land belonging to Hareshaw Farm, it was removed from the crash site by the shepherd from Sundaysight, Walter Melrose. This may have been because the route to Sundaysight would have been easier going.

An attempt was made to recover the aircraft, although because of the boggy conditions this must have been a daunting task. Local memory recalls that a large hole had been dug around the wrecked aircraft which had been suspended on sheer legs within the hole. The plan had then been to winch it clear but torrential rain fell overnight and washed the peat back into the hole, burying the aircraft once more. The recovery of the aircraft was then abandoned.

No court of inquiry was held into the cause of this accident as the RAF concluded that such an inquiry would be unlikely to establish any explanation for the crash at all. F/O , Fisher was not a novice pilot, as he had a total of 337 flying hours with 82 hours completed on Mustangs. But he had done a considerable amount of flying the previous day including some night flying, an activity which demands a great deal of concentration in a single engined fighter. Although the cloud was fairly thick and low that day, the higher points of the moorland were not totally hidden from view. Perhaps F/O Fisher was tired from the exertions of his flying the previous day and let his concentration wander for just a fatal fraction of a second.

At first glance the flight of an aircraft of Army Co-operation Command close to an Army training area would seem a logical and natural event. However, 4 Squadrons records do not show that any training was carried out over the Otterburn Ranges at that period and neither do they show any other flights to Edinburgh. It is strange that the destination of the flight is shown as Edinburgh because there was no RAF establishment known as RAF Edinburgh. The closest airfield would have been

Turnhouse. Was it coincidence that F/O Fisher's parents lived in Edinburgh, and was there some connection between that fact and the reason for the flight? Unfortunately official records contain no answers to these questions and the reasons for AG617's last flight remain unknown. F/O J. Fisher became another addition to the ever growing list of airmen who lost their lives while not confronting the enemy.

Bristol Beaufort IA DX118   24/02/1943

The Bristol Beaufort is one of the lessser known types of aircraft to have flown with the RAF during WW II.

Designed in response to specifications M15/35 and G24/35 which called for a torpedo bomber and general reconnaissance aircraft, the Beaufort made some use of the technology and layout of the Blenheim. However, a crew of three was called for and because of this and the need to carry a torpedo the new aircraft became too heavy and large for the power provided by the Mercury engines of the Blenheim. The more powerful Perseus sleeve valve radial engine of 900 h.p. was substituted to restore performance to the aircraft. However, the Air Ministry in its wisdom decided that the aircraft should have a fourth crew member and a larger fuselage in order to carry a heavier weapons load. This new requirement was covered by specification 10/36. But more power would be needed and the Perseus engines were replaced by the 14 cylinder, 2 row-radial Taurus sleeve-valved engine. Blackburn, who were designing the Botha to fulfil the same specifications, and along parallel lines to the Beaufort, did not re-engine their aircraft and as a result the Botha had a very lack lustre performance.

The prototype of the Beaufort first flew on 15/10/1938. It was a twin engined monoplane of stressed metal skin construction. Very few problems could have been encountered during development of the type as it entered service with 22 Squadron, RAF, in November 1939. In the meantime Bristol had included some of the parts of the Beaufort in the design of the Beaufighter, which was destined to be built in far larger numbers and have a more significant impact on the air war than the Beaufort. Nevertheless, the Beaufort was a competent aircraft. It did not serve with many U.K. based squadrons, most of its operational career being in the Middle and Far East.

The aircraft based in the UK were used mostly in attacks against shipping using both torpedoes and bombs while those that served in the Middle and Far East were also employed, in addition, as medium bombers against land targets. The nature of the operations they took part in were mostly humdrum and routine. Because it was seldom used on those missions which got into the limelight the Beaufort, and its crews, never received much publicity, either during or after the war. There can be little doubt however, that both aircraft and crews made a significant contribution to the war effort.

Some Beauforts were built with Pratt and Whitney engines, and it was this version which was licence-built in Australia, as the Pratt and Whitney engine was more readily available there. Total production of Beauforts was about 2000.

DX118 was a Mk IA version of the Beaufort, the major difference between this version and the original Mk I being the substitution of slightly more powerful and improved Taurus XII engines. The aircraft was destined to have a very short career in the RAF when it was delivered to 44 MU at RAF Edzelll on 21/01/1943. RAF Edzell was situated a few miles to the north-west of Montrose on the east coast of Scotland. When DX 118 was delivered there one of 44 MU's tasks was the conversion of Beauforts modified for tropical use back to a standard temperate torpedo-bomber configuration.

This work complete DX 118 was ready for delivery to its first unit. This was to be 5 OTU stationed at RAF Long Kesh in Northern Ireland. On 23/02/1943 Flight Offfficer W.B.L. Milton of the Air Transport Auxilary (ATA) arrived at Edzell to fly the aircraft to Northern Ireland. William Byrd Lee Milton, of Hopewell Virginia USA was nominally based at RAF Kirkbride with 16 Ferry Pilots Pool(FPP). William Milton was unusual as a pilot in that he was an ordained priest. His brother, Marshall, was also a priest and they were the Ministers of the Episcopalian Church in the adjoining parishes of Hopewell and Brandon, Virginia. They also shared another calling, and that was to fly. They both decided to help the allied cause and enlisted in the Ferry Pilot service.

The Air Transport Auxiliary was only loosely affiliated to the RAF and was responsible for the ferrying and delivering of new and repaired aircraft. Most of its pilots were volunteers and many were women. They were often asked to fly aircraft for ferry purposes which they had never flown before and usually had no training for. Their only recourse was to read the pilot's notes assiduously before take-off. In addition they could sometimes be asked to fly aircraft single handed which, normally, in operational use, would have had further crew members. To lessen the risk to themselves and the aircraft ATA pilots were instructed to always fly below the clouds and to keep the ground in view at all times. This made flying in hilly areas particularly hazardous but flights through such areas were normally accomplished by following valleys.

66

It is therefore likely that F/O Milton was over the Border Hills on Tuesday 23/02/43 in an attempt to use the Tyne Valley gap as a safe low level route to traverse the hills of Northern England. Certainly a straight line between Edzell and Long Kesh would not have brought the aircraft anywhere near the eastern Border area where it met its fate. At some point in time during the flight the starboard engine failed. F/O Milton did all he could to keep the aircraft flying but the Beaufort had a reputation of being a "tricky" aircraft to fly and its single-engined performance was described as "critical". Unfortunately William Milton's' efforts were to no avail and DX 118 struck a hilltop 1 mile to the west of Makendon between 12:00 and 14:00. There is no more accurate time for the crash than that. Makendon , a small hill farm, stands at the head of the infant River Coquet. The Beaufort crashed on a gentle rounded hill about ½ mile due east of the Roman camp remains at Chew Green. The aircraft caught fire and William Milton was killed instantly.

A guard of RAF personnel was sent to guard the wreckage and these men were billeted at Fulhope, another farm, slightly lower down the Coquet Valley.

The ensuing inquiry must have been very through, for it found that immediately prior to the crash all controls were set in the correct position for singled engined flight on the port engine. These controls included the trimmers and starboard propeller pitch set to full coarse. The report of the inquiry absolved F/O Milton of any blame for the accident. The record also shows that he only had 5 hours of experience of flying Beauforts.

Sometime before the crash the Archbishop of Canterbury had given William Milton special dispensation to help in the Diocese of Bristol and as a result he had preached in the Cathedral there several times.

Willaim Milton was cremated and his ashes returned to his family in the U.S.A Over a four year period, including 1943, the ATA had an average fatality of 22%. Not only combat flying was dangerous.

Only a month after the crash of DX118, in early April, all 5 0TU's Beauforts were grounded because of persistent engine failures. This was subsequently found to be due to oil starvation and was not cured until all the aircraft's engines had an improved oil pipe fitted. Could this also have been the problem with DX 118?.

De Havilland Tiger Moth   **N9462**   **01/03/1943**

With a design that dated back to 1925 when the first Moth flew, the Tiger Moth seemed like an anachronism even at the start of World War

II. And yet it was quintessentially British. Even now it is remembered almost equally as well as some of the very famous combat aircraft such as the Spitfire and Lancaster.

It was a bi-plane, little different in design to those aircraft which the RAF had been using at the end of World War I. Powered by a De Havilland Gypsy Major engine of 130 h.p. the Tiger Moth's maximum speed was 109 m.p.h. It was used as a primary trainer by the RAF from the early 1930s, through World War II, before being phased out of service in the late 1940's. The vast majority of British and Dominion pilots of World War II would have made their first flight in a Tiger Moth. The type was also used by the USAAF (C) where it was known as the PT-24. Altogether almost 9,000 were built including those produced in Canada, Australia, and New Zealand. The remainder were built in the United Kingdom, where most of the war-time production was entrusted to Morris Motors at Cowley.

First delivered to 19 MU on 03/12/1939, N9462 was stored for some time before being issued to 30 EFTS at Derby on 21/11/1940. It was returned to 19 MU on 05/03/1941, possibly for some kind of minor repair, and was then reissued to 17 EFTS based at North Luffenham, Rutland on 13/03/1941. Some time later in 1941, possibly in May, consideration was given to transferring the aircraft to 25 (Polish) FTS at nearby Peterborough airfield but apparently this was never carried out, the next move being to 15 EFTS at Kingstown, Carlisle on 24/05/1942.

There was a moderate west south west wind blowing at Kingstown on 01/03/1942 when Sgts V.G. Dickens and E.W. Stevenson climbed aboard N9462 and took off for a map reading flight. The sky was overcast and visibility was only moderate. The aircraft did not return when expected, and when, after more time had elapsed it had not returned at all it was posted missing at 13:00 hours. It was not to be heard of again at Kingstown until 04/03/1943.

Sometime on 03/03/1943 the shepherd from Paddaburn, Willie Hogarth, had been making his rounds and had reached a point at the northernmost extremity of Paddaburn land. The boundary here between Paddaburn and the neighbouring farm, High Cranecleugh, was ill defined and no boundary wall existed. This boundary ran along the crest of a ridge of hills which form the watershed of the River North Tyne and the River Irthing. High Cranescleugh Farm lay on the northeastern slope of this ridge approximately 6 miles west of the village of Falstone, which is situated in the North Tyne Valley. The only way to keep the two sheep stocks apart was to regularly drive them down the hill away from the boundary area and then allow them to instinctively move slowly back up the hill. This process not only ensured that the two flocks did not mix but also forced the ewes to make use of the whole hill for grazing rather than just sticking to the sweeter, lusher, and more sheltered areas. This was herding in the true sense of the word. Having reached this point Willie noticed a feature on High Cranecleugh's land just to the north east of Sighty Crag which he could not remember having seen before. Curious, he went to take a closer look and discovered the crumpled remains of an aircraft. The aircraft had obviously flown directly into the hillside as the engine was embedded in the ground. Immediately behind the engine the fuselage had broken through and the after part of the aircraft propelled by its own momentum had then looped over, coming to rest inverted virtually above the engine. One of the occupants was already dead but the other man was still alive although quite badly injured. The aircraft he had found was N9462.

High Cranecleugh at that time was farmed by Willy and Nancy Anderson. There were three young sons, Matthew, Brian and Robert. Knowing that High Cranescleugh was much closer to the crashed aircraft than Paddaburn, and that he would need help to carry the injured airman to safety, and much needed treatment, Willie made for there as rapidly as possible. Once there he quickly made the Andersons aware of the situation. Willie Hogarth and Mr Anderson returned to the crash site with the underframe from a bed. On reaching the crash site they gently lifted the injured airman, Sgt Dickens, on to the bedframe and using it as a stretcher, carried him down to the house at High Cranescleugh. This was a journey of approximately 1 ¾ to 2 miles over descending moorland. They had tied a rope to each end of the bed and each man put this rope around his neck and shoulders to help support the inJured man's weight whilst traversing the tussock grass. Even without carrying anything walking is difficult over this type of ground. But they eventually arrived at High Cranescleugh.

With Sgt Dickens now safely at the house Mrs. Anderson assessed that he needed urgent medical attention. There was no telephone and as she considered her priority should be to look after the inJured airman she decided to send her son Matthew, aged 5 ½ , down to Low Cranecleugh with a hand written note asking for medical assistance. Hew, as Matthew was known was instructed to run as fast as he could, for Sgt Dickens condition appeared to be serious. Mrs Anderson could not send either of her other sons as Brian, although at home was no more than a toddler and Robert boarded away from home with his grandmother at Eals in order that he could attend school at The Hott on a daily basis. The journey must have been quite an adventure for the young Hew as no road existed between High and Low Cranecleugh but he arrrived safely. Low Cranecleugh was farmed by Willy Anderson's two brothers, Robert and Newby and was situated approximately 2½ miles east of High

Cranecleugh, on the Cranecleugh Burn. There was still no telephone line here, but at least there was a road. But the Andersons did not possess a car and in order to get the message to Doctor Kirk at Bellingham Robert, who had been spreading manure, cycled there, a distance of about seven miles. Doctor Kirk immediately proceeded to Low Cranescleugh by car. He then used one of the Anderson's fell ponies to make his way out to High Cranescleugh in order to treat Sgt. Dickens. The authorities involved, that is the police and via them the RAF, were informed at about the same time and arrangements were made to collect Sgt. Dickens and take him to hospital. The absence of any form of road between High and Low Cranescleugh meant that Sgt. Dickens had to make the first part of his journey on a sledge pulled by one of the Low Crancleugh ponies.

Having got Sgt. Dickens to Low Crancleugh he was then taken by ambulance to the City General (EMS), Hospital Carlisle, where he slowly recovered from his injuries.

A Court of Inquiry was held on 17/03/1943 into the possible causes of the crash and this was presided over by S/L K.C. Baker of 4 EFTS. F/Lt D. M. Crook DFC of 15 EFTS was also a member of this inquiry team. By this time it had been established that Sgt Dickens had been flying the aircraft and Sgt Stevenson was described as a "passenger". The Court of Inquiry concluded that Sgt. Dickens had made an Error of Judgement in that he had failed to accurately monitor his position while climbing through layers of cloud. He had then descended through cloud to establish his position and this was considered unnecessary as apparently there were adequate gaps in the cloud through which he could have checked his position. The aircraft crashed into the hillside whilst still descending in the cloud. With the benefit of hindsight this judgement seems a little harsh as the document recording the conclusion of this Court of Inquiry also shows that Sgt Dickens had only 98 hours of flying in his log book with only 17 hours of that time being solo. This was not a lot of experience and as with most other acquired skills, increase of experience of flying would have undoubtedly led to better judgement.

When N9462 struck the hillside, with terminal results, it had completed 786 hours of flying. Its shattered remains were removed using a similar if not the same sledge which had carried Sgt Dickens on the first stage of his journey to hospital.

Note:- Records use two spellings for Sgt Dickens – Dickins also being used.

Vickers Wellington Ic   X3171   01/02/1943

The crash of this Wellington serves as an almost perfect example of how localised any civilian knowledge of these events was —— and how isolated each individual community was from another. This Wellington, as described in the "Background", crashed on exactly the same day as Tiger Moth N9462 and while there is strong recollection of the events surrounding the crash of the Tiger Moth by one group of people, there is barely any recollection at all of the Wellington crash. A very small number of people can remember a large aircraft crashing in the area mentioned in official records of the crash but nobody can be found who can pinpoint the exact location of the impact. And it should be remembered that a distance of only 9 or 10 miles, as the crow flies, separates the two crash sites.

One of the major official documents recording this crash has also confused, and misled, numerous people over the years in that it shows an incorrect serial number for the aircraft involved. In any publication up to the present which mentions this crash in any way, and they are very few, the aircraft involved is identified as Wellington Ic R3173. Unfortunately, that particular aircraft survived until 1947 and no other Wellingtons in the R317—range have records which show them as having been lost to any cause in March 1943. This accident record does show, however, that whatever the true identity of the aircraft was it was serving with 15 OTU on the day it crashed. It also shows the pilot of the aircraft to have been a Sgt D.L. Barley. Operational records of 15 OTU reveal that the aircraft flown by Sgt Barley on 01/03/1943, and which subsequently crashed, to have been Wellington Ic X3171.

Although X3171 was never operated by an operational squadron it did have an unusual and interesting early career. First delivered to 23 MU on 03/03/1941 the aircraft's first flying unit was 3 PRU (Photographic Reconnaissance Unit) who took it on charge on 20/04/1941. However only three days later it was delivered to the Royal Aircraft Establishment (RAE) at Farnborough under the auspices of the Director General of Research and Development of the RAF. What research the aircraft was involved in is not known, but on 21/07/1941 it was transferred to the Aeroplane and Armament Experimental Establishment (A&AEE) at Martlesham Heath. Whilst there it underwent repairs which were carried out by Vickers on 20/09/1941. Once again it is not known what duties the aircraft performed at the A&AEE. The aircraft went into storage at 10 MU on 26/10/1941 and was not re-issued until 06/03/1942 when 15 OTU at RAF Harwell took it on charge. During its service with 15 OTU it suffered two minor accidents which necessitated it being repaired at Vickers'

Weybridge works, the first time on 11/05/1942 and the second time on 18/08/1942.

On the night of 01—02/06/1942 RAF Bomber Command mounted its second 1000 bomber raid, the target being Essen. All available serviceable aircraft were pressed into use, as were any crews at OTUs who were deemed competent enough to carry out the operation. As a result of this X3171 was used on this raid and was flown by a crew captained by F/Sgt. A.R. Middleton. The aircraft returned unscathed, although the raid itself was not considered to have been such a success as the similar one of the previous night on Cologne.

On 01/03/1943 X3171 took off on what is described as a "solo training flight". The crew consisted of Pilot, Sgt D.L. Barley, Bomb Aimer, P/O J. Donnely, 2nd Bomb Aimer, P/O T. Winstanley. Air Gunner, Sgt G. Marshall, Navigator Sgt W.S. Gibson and Wireless Operator/Air Gunner Sgt D. R. Bendings. They took off at about 11:00 hours. Nothing more is known about the flight only that it ended in their aircraft diving vertically into the ground from cloud at approx. 15:15. The site of the crash is described as Blackburn Fell, 9 miles north-west of Bellingham. Nobody still alive today (1998) can remember the exact site of the crash but a few people can vaguely recollect an aircraft crashing on the moorland approximately half a mile due west of Ridley Shiel. This area is shown on older maps as Blackburn Common. It is assumed that X3171 was this aircraft.

In such a crash, with its resulting fire, the crew had no chance of survival and all perished. The pilot, Sgt Barley was quite inexperienced having completed only 186 hours of flying. With only 18 hours of this total spent flying Wellingtons together with the description of the flight as "solo training fight" it is possible that this was the first time he had had sole control of a Wellington.

The report on the accident surmises that the pilot lost control of the aircraft whilst flying in cloud. Many bomber crews considered that the OTU phase of their training was the most dangerous part of their wartime experiences, indeed it was often joked that if you survived OTU then it was very likely that you would survive the war. Unfortunately for many aircrews this was to be far from the truth. As if to emphasise the risks involved at OTUs the ORB for 15 OTU for the month of March 1943 records that 3 other Wellingtons crashed during that month with a total loss of aircrew (including the crew of X3171) of 16 airmen. Sobering facts, especially when one considers that these were the statistics for just one OTU for just one month.

German Aircraft 24-25/03/1943

The events of the night of 24-25/03/1943 must have been a bitter blow for the Luftwaffe, for of the 25 of their aircraft despatched to attack Edinburgh 8 failed to return to their bases.

Of these 8 aircraft, 4 came to grief in the Border Area. Events surrounding the crashes of two of these aircraft, Dornier 217E-4 (Werke Nr 5432 – coded U5+DL) and Junkers 88A-14 (Werke Nr 144354 – coded 3E+BH) have been previously described in "Where the Hills Meet the Sky". However further information has now been found which throws a different light on some of the events of the night.

One of the aircraft lost that night was a Dornier 217E-4 (Werke Nr 4365 –coded U5+FR) of 7/KG-2. It suffered an engine failure and 3 of the crew baled out before it crashed in the hills of Kirkcudbrightshire. Subsequent interrogation of this crew revealed that the mission had started from airfields in Holland and after using the Den Helder light as a navigational reference point had flown across the North Sea at an altitude of 150 feet in attempt to escape detection by radar. At a point approximately 90 miles east of St Abbs Head the aircraft obtained a D/F position fix from a transmitter located at Stavanger in Norway. Having accurately plotted their position the aircraft then climbed to a slightly higher altitude and made inland. At this point the crews had been instructed to alter their courses every 90 seconds in an attempt to prevent the radar equipped British nightfighters from detecting them. These nightfighters, mostly Beaufighters, had become very successful and the Luftwaffe high command obviously regarded them with a great deal of respect and trepidation. This instruction to alter course so frequently did, however, pose a problem for the crews, in that they were navigating by Dead-Reckoning and the frequency of the course changes meant that the navigator did not have enough time to calculate his new position at each course alteration. This inevitably led to some aircraft being off there intended track and to others being totally lost. Other aircraft, in an attempt to keep track of their position, probably ignored the instruction to zig-zag, but in keeping to a steadier course put themselves in danger of being detected and attacked.

The Luftwaffe aircraft involved that night were all Dornier 217E-4s of KG2 or Junkers 88A-14s of KG6. The aircraft of KG2 were based in Holland but those of KG6 were based in Northern France and had first flown to Deelen in Holland to replenish their fuel tanks in order that they would have enough range to complete the mission.

The Dornier 217 was a development of the earlier Dornier 17 bomber. It had first flown in 1938 and had entered operational service in mid 1940. The E series first entered service in late 1940 with the E-4 sub-type starting operations in mid 1941. The Dornier 217E-4 was powered by two BMW 801C 14 cylinder radial engines of 1580 h.p. This was a very advanced air cooled engine and had an installed drag factor less than some in-line liquid cooled engines of comparable power and gave the Dornier 217E-4 a good enough performance for it to be operated as a night fighter as well as a medium bomber.

The Ju88s involved in this mission were similar to the one described earlier in this guide (Werke Np 7122-VB+KM) except that they were of the A-14 sub-type.

The A-14 sub-type was designed to operate at low altitude and to assist in this role was equipped with barrage balloon cable cutters, from which it acquired the name Kuto-Nase (Cutting Nose) and was also equipped with FuG 101 which was an early, crude form of radio altimeter. The aircraft was powered by two Junkers Juno 211J inverted V-12 liquid cooled engines of 1410 h.p.

In "Where the Hills Meet the Sky" it is conjectured that the Luftwaffe aircraft attacked and subsequently brought down by Beaufighter X6879 of 409 Squadron was not the one which the crew of Pilot S/L G. Elms and Radar Operator F/O J.D. Hore-Keinnard later claimed as having shot down. This aircraft, that is the one they claimed, was the Ju 88 (144354) which crashed at Linhope Rigg. The aircraft which is suggested was the one brought down by them was the Dornier 217 (Werke Nr 5432) which crashed at Madam Law, near Trowupburn. Further study of RAF Fighter Command combat reports and monthly returns of enemy aircraft lost, plus intelligence reports completed as a result of investigations of crash sites, make it clear that this theory was certainly not the case. In fact another Ju88A-14 (Werke Nr 144550- coded 3E + MN) crashed 4 miles east of Earlston in Berwickshire and since the attack byX6879 had taken place within minutes of the crash it was the destruction of this aircraft which the 409 Squadron crew were eventually credited with. In fact many people can still remember the crash of this aircraft. Not only that but they also remember the attacks which caused the crash. This Ju88 was operated by II/KG6 based at Cormeilles-en-Vexin. The crew consisted of Oberentnant Paul Rogge, Unteroffizier Ernst Glick, Unteroffizier K. Brinkmann and Unteroffizier W. Walter who all lost their lives when the aircraft crashed. The confusion regarding this aircraft may have arisen because its crash was reported by the Berwickshire police who consequently informed their nearest RAF Station which would have been Charter Hall. In the ensuing delay of this information reaching Fighter Command or Group HQ, 409 Squadron of Acklington had already claimed the Linhope Rigg aircraft, which was of course nearer to them.

74

"Where the Hills Meet the Sky" also postulated that the Ju88 which crashed at Linhope Rigg may have been the aircraft attacked and damaged by Beaufighter V8555 of 219 Squadron. This aircraft was being flown by P/O Robinson with Sgt Hartley as radar operator. The crew actually identified the aircraft they attacked as a Dornier 217 and another aircraft of this type did crash in the Border area that night. This was Do 217E (Werke Nr 1182- coded U5+KP) of IV/KG2 based at Soesterberg in Holland. The aircraft crashed on Steele Rigg, about half a mile north of "Twice Brewed Inn" and close to Hadrian's Wall. The crash occurred at 0030 (half past midnight) and local recall suggests that it had dropped some bombs at Sewingshields, about 3 miles to the east, just before this crash. It could have been jettisoning these bombs as there are also reports that the Luftwaffe aircraft was being pursued and fired at by a British night fighter. This report is from local recall and is confirmed by a Fighter Command Intelligence report which records an attack on this aircraft by a nightfighter at 00:15 hours. The Do 217E-4 distintegrated on impact and the crew consisting of Leutnant Rudolf Frase, Unteroffizier Willi Scneider, Oberefreiter Alois Ille, and Gefreiter S. Hartz were all killed.

Several months after these events a Fighter Command monthly return of enemy aircraft losses (backdated) concluded that only 1 of the Luftwaffe aircraft which crashed that night had done so as a result of an attack by a nightfighter and that was the Ju88 at Earlston.

One\other Luftwaffe aircraft, a Ju88, which crashed at Hare Hill 7 miles south of Edinburgh was credited to an Anti Aircraft Battery based in Balerno.

The crashes of all the other aircraft that night, including those at Linhope Rigg, Trowupburn, and Steele Rigg are attributed to "other causes".

And therefore no conclusion can be drawn about the ultimate fate of the aircraft attacked and damaged by Beaufighter V8555.

Avro Lancaster II D50650   03/03/1944

There can be very few people, even among those who do not have interest in aircraft, who have not heard of the Avro Lancaster. It was one of the most famous and charismatic British war time aircraft and literally became a legend in its own lifetime.

Originally developed to meet the requirements of Specification P13/36, which also gave rise to the Halifax, the type, which was then known as the Manchester, evolved around the use of the highly complex and untried Rolls-Royce Vulture X-24 liquid cooled engine. This engine proved to be less powerful than expected and suffered from huge serviceablity problems most of which were associated with incurable overheating problems. The Manchester airframe, however was very sound and the aircraft entered squadron service in December 1940. Because of the poor engine performance and equally poor reliability of these engines it suffered heavy losses. In an attempt to improve its' performance and reliability the type was eventually re-engined with 4 Rolls-Royce Merlins and this proved to be an instant success. The resultant aircraft was so different that it was renamed Lancaster. It inherited the immensely strong bomb-bay floor of the Manchester, which had been bestowed on that aircraft by the Air-Ministries insistence that it should be capable of being launched by catapult. The bomb bay floor had been the attachment point for the catapult mechanism hence its strength. This feature was to be critical to the Lancaster's later success when it was asked to carry not only larger and larger bomb loads but also extremely large single bombs. The Lancaster became an immediate success. It was so successful that very few different Marks had to be developed. Such that there were only differed from the MkI in having different engines. This was done so as to avoid aircraft being prevented from being completed due to a shortage of engines. Hence the Mk III had American built Packard Merlins and the Mk X was a Canadian built version of the MkIII.

DS650, however was quite an unusual aircraft in that it was one of only 300 aircraft produced which utilised 4 Bristol Hercules 14 cylinder radial aircooled engines in place of the Merlins. These were designated Lancaster II. The Mark II Lancaster was only operated by six RAF Squadrons, and three of these were Canadian Squadrons of 6 Group, Bomber Command. The Mark II quickly gained a reputation amongst those who flew it as possibly being the best "Lanc" of all. With a 20% increase in power over its Merlin engined stablemates, it could climb more quickly, cruise at a higher speed, take off more rapidly and had a higher maximum speed. It did, however, have a few drawbacks. Amongst these was its far higher fuel consumption which was a major problem in that it reduced the types range and therefore its operational usefulness. That it was not able to operate at quite the same altitude as the Merlin engined versions was not quite so important but nevertheless reduced its usefulness. Perversely, when the MkII was phased out of operational service the Squadrons that operated it were converted to the Mk III Halifax. This was perceived, questionably, to be an inferior aircraft to the Lancaster but the conversion was carried out because the Halifax III also utilised the Hercules engine and it was thought the conversion would be easier because all members of these Squadrons, air crew and ground crew alike, were familiar with the new aircraft's engines. It did not occur to anyone that the rest of the aircraft was totally different!!

DS650, like all 300 Lancaster IIs was built by Armstrong-Whitworth and delivered to 426 Squadron at RAF Linton-on-Ouse, on 12/06/1943. This squadron was a member of 6 Group Bomber Command, and its personnel were mostly Canadians serving with the RCAF. The Squadron had up to this time been operating MkIII Wellingtons but in June/August 1943 became the first RCAF squadron to receive to receive the new and unusual Mark of Lancaster.

The aircrews of 426 Squadron must have spent most of late June, July, and early August in training to convert to the Lancasters and no operational fights were undertaken. However, on 30/08/1943, DS650 took part in a mission to Munchen Gladbach and was flown by a crew captained by Sgt L.P. Archibold. The following day, 31/08/1943, the aircraft took off on a mission whose target was Berlin. On this occasion the aircraft was flown by a crew captained by F/O L.N. McCaig. Unfortunately the mission had to be aborted due to the engines overheating and the aircraft being unable to climb above 14,000 feet. Engine management on these Mk II Lancasters was fairly tricky and a balance had to be struck between throttle settings and cooling gill opening. It was not unusual to be able to fly faster at less than full throttle than it was at full throttle. This was because at full throttle the cooling gills had to be fully open to avoid overheating but this in turn induced a large amount of drag which impaired the aircraft's performance. DS650 returned safely to Linton –on- Ouse having jettisoned its 4000LB bomb. On 02/09/1943, DS650 made its final operational flight. This was a mining operation with the mines to be dropped in the area around the Frisian Islands. The aircraft was flown by Sgt J.A.R. Coulmee and returned to base having successfully completed the mission with nothing untoward having occurred.

On 09/10/1943 DS650 was transferred to 1679 Conversion Unit at RAF East Moor. This airfield, as noted in the story of Mustang AG617, was located just to the east of York and within a few miles of Linton-on-Ouse. The airfield was occupied at this time by 432 Squadron another Canadian Squadron who were operating Wellington X's. They were, however, about to convert to Lancaster II's. At the end of September a new crew, captained by F/O Jim McIntosh was posted into 432 Squadron. They only flew a couple of operational missions with Wellingtons before they transferred sideways to 1679 CU. This was to convert them to operating the Lancaster II. On 15/11/1943 Jim McIntosh made his second Lancaster II flight in DS650 and subsequently flew it on three more training flights. By the end of November they were passed as operationally ready and transferred back to 'B' Flight of 432 Squadron.

Some time in January 1944, 1679 CU moved to RAF

Wombleton, an airfield in East Yorkshire. Not long after it changed its identity and became 1660 Heavy Conversion Unit (HCU). It did, however, remain in Group 6.

On Friday 03/03/1944. DS 650, now coded ND-P took off at 1845 hours from Wombleton on a "Bullseye" exercise. These exercises were not only training flights for the crew but were also intended to provide training for the air defence organisations in that they simulated attacks on targets. The crew for this exercise consisted of Pilot and Captain P/O R.G. Calder (RCAF), Navigator F/S R.W. Cambell (RCAF), Bomb Aimer Sgt J. A. Simms (RCAF), Wireless Operator W.O.2 F.J. Leech(RCAF),Flight Engineer Sgt R. Bell (RAF), Mid Upper Gunner Sgt J. Speight (RAF) and Rear Gunner Sgt R.C. Gibbs (RAF.)

Around 10 o'clock that evening Dick Dunn, a forestry worker who was living with his mother near Byrness just to the east of the Catcleugh Reservoir, was about to go to bed , as he was due to be at work early the following morning, Saturday 4th March. It was then that he heard the howl of a diving large aircraft. The sound rapidly increased into a frightening roar. Dick rushed outside and immediately saw a large aircraft at low attitude making straight for his house. This aircraft was obviously in trouble for an engine seemed to be on fire and pieces appeared to be falling away from it. Fearful that the aircraft might indeed crash into the house he called his mother and told her to get outside and away from the house as quickly as possible. The aircraft was travelling in a north westerly direction up Redesdale and fortunately did not hit Dick's house and he and his mother watched it narrowly miss the Byrness Hotel and then crash into the hillside immediately to the north of and behind the Hotel. It burst into flames and for DS650 the Bullseye Exercise had ended. The following morning the normally tranquil area was a hive of activity with RAF personnel busy at the crash site and along the valley of the River Rede. Pieces of wreckage were found for quite a considerable distance along the valley with part of the tail assembly including a fin being found at Blakehopeburnhaugh approximately 2 ½ miles south of where DS650 had finally and violently come to rest. It became apparent that the aircraft must have been breaking up in mid-air and some of the unfortunate crew had been spilt out along the same line as the trail of wreckage. Three bodies were discovered near the two unusual octagonal shaped houses known as the Inkpots, which stand to the west of the A68 trunk road about a mile to the south east of Byrness. Another body was found near Rawfoot Bridge. There had been a hard frost that night and where each body lay an inprint of it was found in the frosted ground. It is thought that two bodies were found in the wreckage at the crash site although this cannot be confirmed but if true would leave one body unaccounted for. Sadly the whole crew

78

had perished and the seventh body must have been found for over the next few days funerals took place at several places throughout Britain. P/O Calder was buried in Edinburgh on 08/03/1944. Although serving in the RCAF his wife is recorded as being from Edinburgh. The three other members of the RCAF were buried at Stonefall Cemetery, Harrogate on 10/03/1944 whilst the funerals of Sgt Bell, Sgt Speight and Sgt Gibbs took place on 09/03/1944 at Newcastle, Pontefract and Bristol respectively. All of these funerals were attended by an officer from 1666 HCU to represent the RAF.

An investigation by the RAF into the cause of the crash concluded that the pilot lost control of the aircraft which then subsequently started to dive at an ever increasing speed. This speed eventually became so great that the stress on the aircraft's structure increased beyond design limits and structural failure resulted. No reason is given or suggested for the pilot loosing control but P/O Calder was a reasonably experienced pilot with over 300 hours of flying in his log-book. With that number of hours it is possible that he may even have flown some operational missions. (See notes in "Sources" for explanation of why this would be difficult to establish). It is known that as good an aircraft as the Lancaster was that it did suffer from some structural defects. One of these defects was the loss of the fabric covering from the elevators on the tail structure, and this event would have resulted in a similar loss of control of the aircraft. The investigation also records that the witnesses reported having seen gunfire. The word "they" is used in this section of the report and it therefore follows that more than one person must have reported seeing it. The official investigation report, however, dismisses these claims as unsubstantiated. Might it just be possible, in view of the fact that more than one person reported it, that there was some gunfire and that perhaps this had come either from the nearby Otterburn Ranges or an undetected British nightfighter. After all the aircraft had been on a "Bullseye Exercise" of which one objective was to challenge the British defences. All of this is, of course, pure conjecture and the only man who knew the exact answer to the conundrum lost his life that night together with six of his crewmen.

Handley Page Halifax II Series Ia JP190   01/04/1944

The tiny hamlet of Craik lies at the head of Borthwick Water about 11 miles west of Hawick. It is a remote and tranquil place and its nearest neighbours are a few scattered and equally remote upland farms nestling in the valley of the Borthwick Water. About 1¾ miles due west of

Craik is the isolated shepherd's house at Wolfcleuchhead. It stands close by the Wolfcleuch Burn, a tributary of Bothwick Water, where that infant stream skirts around the northern shoulder of the 1400 foot hill, Muckle Knowe.

On the night of the 01/04/1944 the peace and tranquillity of this almost idyllic setting was shattered in a dramatic way. At 23:30 the shepherd at Wolfcleuchhead, Alexander Reid, was startled by the sound of a low flying, and obviously very large aircraft approaching his house. He went outside and caught sight of the aircraft flying very low in a westerly direction with an engine on fire. Suddenly it dived and struck the northern side of Muckle Knowe. There was a bright flash followed by a very loud explosion. Mr Reid immediately set out for the crash site, which was about ½ mile west of his house. He was joined by William Moffat, who farmed Craich Farm. When the two men got to the crash site it was a scene of utter devastation with wreckage spread over a wide area. They found 3 bodies that night with another 5 bodies being found the following morning by a special team organised by Sgt Wood, of Hawick Police. F/Sgt Alan Franks had arrived from RAF Charter Hall to take charge of the scene on behalf of the RAF and it was he who arranged for the casualties to be taken to Charter Hall.

The aircraft that had crashed was Handley Page Halifax II Series Ia JP190. It was built by the London Aircraft Production Group sometime in late November 1943. Destined to be among the last batches of Merlin powered Halifaxs to be built it had all the aerodynamic refinements such as the streamlined nose and the modified rectangular fins which had become a feature of later aircraft.

It was allocated to 1656 HCU based at RAF Lindholme, near Doncaster, on 06/01/1944. It appears to have had an uneventful career up until the night of 01/04/1944. That night it took off from Lindholme at around 20:15 for a cross-country training flight. The crew consisted of Pilot and Captain F/O R.E.Ross. Bomb Aimer, F/O J. Birkett, Navigator F/S P. Burchell, Flight Engineer, Sgt C Farthing, Wireless Operator Sgt H.W. Simpson, 2nd Flight Engineer Sgt B A Bell and two(2) Air Gunners Sgts H. Smith and J.G. Hinder. The Pilot F/O Ronald Emerson (Pat) Ross had been awarded the MBE although it is not known what the circumstances of the award being made were. At the age of 31 he was probably at of the upper age limit for training as aircrew. He had completed 180 hours of flying at the time of the accident. Records from the CWGC also show that he was the holder of the Military Medal. Basically an Army gallantry award, it suggests that at one time F/O Ross may have served in the Army and then re-inlisted in the RAF. As already related, he and the other seven members of the crew sadly all died that night.

A subsequent RAF report on the crash gives no clear cut cause for the accident. It suggests that the engine fire, if indeed there ever was one was probably not a contributory factor. The most likely scenario is that the pilot saw the high ground of Muckle Knowe ahead of him, raised the nose of the aircraft to make sure he cleared it and in so doing stalled the aircraft. The Halifax had sudden and vicious stalling characteristics and this would have resulted in the type of sudden dive described by Alexander Reid. The report concludes that if in fact there had been a fire then the captain should have ordered the crew to bale out. They did not and became yet another grim statistic of WW II. A sadder and more poignant feature of that night is that four young women had been made widows as F/O Ross, F./S. Burchell and Sergeants Smith and Simpson were all married men.

Gradually Craik and Borthwick Water returned to their former peacefulness.

Handley Page Halifax III MZ908   19/09/1944

The geographical location of this crash should preclude it from being included in this guide. The crash did not occur on high ground but is significant because it happened in close proximity to one of the few concentrations of population in the Border Area. Nowadays Wooler acclaims itself to be "The Gateway to the Cheviots" and certainly those selfsame hills start to rise on the western flank of the town.

It was hard against these initial slopes that Halifax III MZ908 came to grief on 19/0 9/1944. Its career in the RAF was brief having first been issued to 48 MU six weeks earlier on 07/08/1944. It had been built by English Electric at Salmesbury in Lancashire. It was taken on charge by 429 squadron based at RAF Leeming on 11/08/1944 but was unlikely to have flown any operational flights with them as it was transferred to 408 Squadron at RAF Linton — on - Ouse on 17/08/1944. Once again the aircraft's stay was short and on 08/09/1944, 434 Squadron based at RAF Croft, near Darlington, became its new and final owner. It's short stay with 408 Squadron was probably due to the fact that the Squadron was in the turmoil of converting aircraft types, in this case from Lancaster II to Halifax VII and therefore MZ908 was not needed by them. These three squadrons were all part of 6 Group, Bomber Command. The group's airfields were all located in North Yorkshire and in addition to the squadrons aircrews being Canadian all other personnel were supplied by the RCAF.

On 18/091944 MZ908, now coded WL-0 was one of the aircraft

dispatched by 434 Squadron to bomb Donburg. It's was to be a daylight mission and involved all the squadrons of 6 Group. The crew, consisted of Pilot (and Captain) F/O J.C.Lees, Navigator P/O R.Thompson, Bomb Aimer F/O B. Warr, Wireless Opereator F/O M Stiles, Flight Engineer, Sgt M Bush, Mid Upper Gunner P/O P.Melneczuk and Rear Gunner F/Sgt W. Boyer. This was an all Canadian crew except for Sgt Bush,the Flight Engineer, who was British. This was a standard arrangement in 6 Group, Bomber Command, and was brought about because no facility existed in Canada for the training of flight engineers.

This crew were getting close to the end of their "tour" of operations and most of their previous missions had been carried out in Halifax III LW689 coded WL—A.

The weather was not particularly good and as the mission progressed it deteriorated even further. So much so that after about two hours the operation was aborted and all the aircraft involved were recalled. However the weather had become so bad that it proved impossible to land at some of the 6 Group airfields due to poor visibility.WL-0 was diverted to Tholthope. All of 6 Group's aircraft were now concentrated on to three airfields.

The following day, 19/09/1944 the weather had improved somewhat and it was decided that the previous day's mission should be tried again. So at 1330 WL-O took off from Tholthorpe, intending to attack the same target, Donburg, as on the previous day, and flown by the same crew. Once again, however, after about an hour, the weather closed in and all the aircraft were recalled.

At around 1600 hours WL-0 was over North Northumberland. No reason has been put forward for its presence in that area and it certainly would not have needed to cross the locality to return to its home base of Coft. The aircraft, as described later, certainly did suffer a mechanical problem, but it is not clear from operational records whether this was the reason for its presence in the area. It would seem unlikely that it was, as the mechanical defect from which the aircraft suffered would have resulted in the aircraft not being able to remain airborne for very long and Wooler would have been at least 45 minutes flying time from a logical course which would have returned the aircraft from its point of recall to Croft.

At around 1600 hours the propeller on the starboard outer engine began to overspeed. It would not feather and eventually it sheared off. It spun away but in doing so struck the propeller of the starboard inner engine which also broke off. The aircraft was now at 6,000 feet. A distress call known as a "Darky" was transmitted but no response was received from this. The "Darky" system was one in which all RAF stations kept a

82

radio watch on one single frequency and this was only used by those aircraft in distress. Hence if an RAF station received a message on this frequency the message did not need to be understandable for those receiving it to be aware that somewhere in the locality an aircraft was in distress. But now WL— 0 was flying with asymmetrical power and had received no instructions from the ground. Six(6) of the crew baled out leaving the pilot, F/O Lees, still at the controls. The aircraft continued flying straight and level for a few seconds but then suddenly turned to port and dived into the ground. The aircraft came to earth just to the east of Akeld Manor and about 200 m south of the main Coldstream to Wooler Road (A697) which at that point runs in a due east west direction. The crashing aircraft careered through a hedge demolishing a tree before finally coming to rest, and then caught fire. Sadly F/O Lees was killed.

The crash had occurred at 1615 hours and no doubt due to the proximity of Millfield Airfield RAF personnel were soon on the scene. The aircraft's home base at Croft was informed of the crash at 1650. Because the aircraft was thought to be carrying bombs the main road was closed and nearby houses including those at Bendor were evacuated until the site was made safe.

The following day W/C Dunphy from RAF Middleton St George accompanied by a Mr Fulton of Bristol Aero Engines went to the scene of the accident to inspect the wreckage. Their findings were incorporated in the report on the causes of the crash. The constant speed unit (CSU) of the propeller assembly of the Halifax's Hercules engines was hydraulically controlled. Like most hydraulic systems it had a relief valve to protect it from overloads. On 19/09/1944 this relief valve on WL-0's starboard outer engine had stuck open. This resulted in some bolts in the CSU stretching which ultimately led to loss of control over the pitch of the propeller blades. The propeller then started to overspeed with the dramatic results already related.

But why didn't F/O Lees bale out with the rest of the crew? The official RAF report into the crash does not even pose this question let alone attempt to answer it. Understandable, perhaps, because any answer can only be conjecture. However, with the benefit of hindsight, there are two possible answers which suggest themselves. The first of these is that F/O Lees had seen the small town of Wooler ahead, and had stayed in the stricken aircraft in an attempt to avoid the possibility of a totally abandoned aircraft crashing there. Or had he stayed at the controls of the aircraft to make sure it flew straight and level whilst the rest of his crew baled out, but then when he left the controls to make his own escape the aircraft had immediately gone out of control. The resulting centrifugal and G-forces may then have pinned him inside the diving aircraft making his escape impossible.

However, as on so many other previous occasions, the only witness who could corroborate those theories, lost his life and was unable to do so.

Handley Page Halifax V DK 116   15/10/1944

Before the Second World War Otterstone Lee had the reputation of being the largest farm, with regard to area, in England. The home steading was situated close to the River North Tyne at the eastern end of this large 12,000 acre plus holding. The western boundary of the farm was the Anglo-Scottish Border. Much of the farm's ground lay on Caplestone Fell, a ridge of high ground bounded on the north by the Akenshaw Burn and on the south by the Lewis Burn . These two easterly flowing streams meet at The Forks, a remote house about 2 miles west of the course of the North Tyne River, and form a letter Y lying on its side; the tail being known as the Lewis Burn, which eventually joins the North Tyne about 1 mile north west of Plashetts.

There were two very remote steadings from which the western end of the farm, including Capelstone Fell, were shepherded. Willowbog stood on the Akenshaw Burn about 2 ½ miles west of the Forks while High Long House stood on the Lewis Burn a similar distance both south west of The Forks and due south of Willowbog. In October 1944 the shepherd at Willowbog was Adam Steele, whilst High Long House was occupied by the Waugh family.

At about 17:45 on 15/10/1944 Halifax V, DK116, coded GG-Z of 1667 HCU took off from RAF Sandtoft,an airfield situated just to the west of Scunthorpe in Lincolnshire. Built by Fairey, DK116 was a Series I Mk V Halifax and had first been issued to 1660 HCU based at RAF Swinderby on 04/02/1943. It was transferred to 1667 HCU on 21/11/1943. The purpose of the flight that night was a cross-country training exercise. The captain of the aircraft was the Pilot, P/O H.G. Haddrell, accompanied by his crew of Navigator Sgt J. Mahoney, Flight Engineer, Sgt J. Nielson, Wireless Operator Sgt Hammond, Bomb Aimer Sgt Reid and Air Gunners W/Os G. Symmonds and M.F. James. P/O Hadrell had 480 hours of flying time to his credit, but although obviously not a novice or inexperienced pilot the 24 hours of this total spent flying Halifaxes meant that his knowledge of flying the type would have been limited.

That evening Adam Steele had walked over Capelstone Fell to High Long House. He and the Waugh family were due to play cards, and the trip would also enable him to collect a pair of his wife's clogs which

84

she had left there some days previously . As they played cards a drama began to unfold high above them.

Somewhere over Dumfries at an altitude of 12,000 feet, the crew of DK116 became aware that the port inner engine of their aircraft was on fire. The pilot, P/O Hadrell, asked the Flight Engineer, Sgt Nielsen, to feather the engine. It is very likely that by this time the engine would have ceased to function correctly and the propeller would have, in fact, been turning the engine by a "windmilling" action. The turning engine would still be drawing petrol from the fuel system and thus feeding the fire. The object of feathering the engine (the propeller really) was to turn the blades edge on to the slip stream with the result that the propeller would stop "windmilling" which in turn meant that the engine would become stationary and thus cease to draw petrol into the fire. However, the propeller, was never feathered. Had Sgt Nielsen not heard his captain's request or had the controls to the engine been so severely damaged by the fire that they no longer responded?

Just after ten o'clock Adam Steele decided it was time to make for home at Willowbog. Mr Waugh accompanied him for part of the way, mostly to ensure that he made his way out on to the correct area of the fell that enabled him to take the easiest route to his home. Several miles to the east some residents of Kielder Village noticed the approach of an aircraft from the west, and more alarmingly that a large fire appeared to be burning in one wing, trailing a shower of sparks behind it. It turned almost immediately over Kielder Village and headed back towards the direction it had come from. Adam Steele and his companion were now well up onto the fell. Suddenly they became aware of a low flying aircraft approaching from the direction of Kielder (i.e. the east). The machine was obviously in serious trouble for flames were billowing from it. For a short time they thought the aircraft was going to hit them but it passed over them only to crash into the hillside to the west of them moments later. The violence of the impact was so great that it seemed to shake the ground beneath their feet. The aircraft they had seen was DK116. They then carried on up the hill in a direction which would lead them to where the aircraft was now burning. This was on a hill known as Marven's Pike. They had not travelled a great distance when they heard whistles being blown and almost simultaneously stumbled across an injured man lying in an open drain. He had lost his flying boots and was barefoot. Before long Adam came across two more airmen who appeared to be uninjured. The whistles Adam had heard being blown belonged to the airmen he had now encountered. All airmen were issued with these whistles which were not unlike those used by railway guards or football referees. Their intended purpose was to be used as a means of drawing attention to themselves in the event of having to abandon an aircraft and so that individual members of a crew could make contact with other members of that crew once on the ground. Adam Steele gave his wife's clogs to the airman who had lost his boots and escorted these three airmen back to High Long House, the injured airman's conditions not being serious enough to prevent him walking. The shepherd then re-started his journey to Willowbog. However it cannot be recalled whether Adam Steele actually went via the crash site or direct to Willowbog. In any event official help started to arrive not long after that. This included some Royal Navy personnel from Lewisburn camp. This camp, along with two others, had been set up in the early 1930s as a labour camp for the initial planting work of Kielder Forest. Out of work people were drafted there from the worst unemployment black spots of the North East. Rumour had it that if a place at one of these camps was refused then all unemployment benefit was withdrawn. Little wonder then that these camps soon earned a reputation for homing political extremists. As soon as the war started the camp was handed over to the Royal Navy who used it as a detention centre for those of its number who fell foul of its regulations.

There was no track beyond The Forks and so a considerable amount of walking had to be carried out by these rescue personnel. Sadly their efforts were to be of no avail as Sgt Nielsen, WO Symmonds and WO James had all perished in the crash. The official RAF accident record shows three of the crew as having lost their lives, with one crew member missing, and the other three airmen as survivors. However the 1667 HCU Operational Record Book records that a fourth body was found. The bodies were taken to Willowbog.

No satisfactory answer has ever been suggested as to why three of the crew managed to escape from the doomed aircraft but the other four did not. A theory put forward in the official accident report is that the Rear Gunner was having difficulty in the evacuating his turret and that the pilot remained at the controls in order to give him more time to do so. This however, raises numerous other questions. The rear turret of the Halifax had an independent and self-contained electro-hydraulic power system. Perhaps the electricity supply to this had been cut off by the engine fire leaving the turret paralysed. Even then the turret had a hand winch system for operating it in the event of the power failing and this could have been utilised to bring the turret to its correct position for evacuation. And had the other two crew members stayed on board in an effort to free the rear gunner?

Obviously an order to abandon the aircraft had been given as witnessed by the three members who had parachuted to safety. But was the aircraft as high above the ground as the crew thought it was.

The impression given by the official (but short) accident report is that those members of the crew who had parachuted to safety had done so from an altitude of 12,000 feet. This is obviously not the case otherwise they would not have been found so close to the site of the eventual crash. Additionally all the official reports refer to the incident as having occurred over Dumfriesshire not Northumberland. This suggests, possibly, that the crew of the aircraft did not know their exact position and because of this were not aware of the height of the ground (1,650 feet a.s.l.) immediately below them. They may well have thought that the aircraft still had most of that height to lose before making contact with the ground and hence more time to make their escape. The fact that those who escaped were found so close to the crash site means that they had only just left the aircraft, and it was probably the intention of those remaining to immediately follow them. However, the time remaining for them to do so was much shorter than they thought, as reasoned above, and they failed to make their escape.

As stated previously P/O Haddrell, the captain, had 480 hours of flying in his log book and so was not an inexperienced pilot, although only 24 hours of this total had been spent at the controls of a Halifax. Taking into account the number of hours flying already completed by him it is very probable that P/O Haddrell had already carried out an operational " tour". Because of this likely exposure to the dangers and stresses of operational flying it would seem unlikely that P/O Haddrell, who was 30 years of age, would have been panicked by the circumstances he found himself in. Once more, this would have been another factor which led to the abandonment of the aircraft being left, seemingly, until the last minute.

All of this is of course pure conjecture and sadly only those who perished that night knew the exact circumstances of DK116's final moments. The aircraft had completed 365 hours and 15 minutes of flying when its service career abruptly ended.

De Havilland Tiger Moth T6828 04/11/1944

This Tiger Moth, like N 9462, which crashed on 01/03/1943, was operated by 15 EFTS based at Kingstown. Built by Morris Motors it had been delivered to the RAF at 33MU on 22/10/1941. The first user of the aircraft was 17 EFTS who took it on charge on 01/11/1941. It was transferred to 15 EFTS on 26/05/1942 and from available records seems to have had an incident free career up until 04/11/1944.

On that day the aircraft took off crewed by Pilot, Sgt F. Palmer and Navigator Sgt R.M.Medwin. The purpose of the flight was a "Wind

Finding Exercise" and the crew had been instructed to stay within the local flying area for Kingstown. There was a south westerly wind of 20 to 25 mph and cloud cover was 9/10 ^{ths}, these not being ideal conditions for flying over high ground. The aircraft did not return and was posted missing. A search party was set up and after a difficult and extensive search in what the 15 EFTS ORB describes as "harsh conditions" the wreckage of the aircraft was eventually found. It is not clear whether the aircraft was found on the same day or perhaps the next day but it had certainly been found by 06/11/1944 as that was the day when a Court of Inquiry into the crash was set up under the chairmanship of S/L F.H. Hawes of 11 EFTS. Unfortunately both of the crew had been killed in the crash but because of the difficulties of the terrain it was not possible to recover their bodies until 07/11/1944.

The crash is stated to have occurred at 1315 hours but it is not made clear how this time was arrived at. There was no evidence of eye witnesses to substantiate this time and it can only be assumed that the time stated was that shown by a timepiece which ceased functioning at the moment of impact. Sgt Palmer (some records spell this name as Pelmer) was not a totally novice pilot and had accumulated 129 hours of flying when he was tragically killed. It was supposed that the crew had lost their position due to the low cloud and rain and then flown into the high ground in conditions of poor visibility. The crash site was five miles outside the limits of local flying for Kingstown.

RAF records report the crash as having occurred in the county of Cumberland, at a place known as Glen Dhu in the Bewcastle Fells area. The hill known as Glendhu is actually in the county of Northumberland and the Bewcastle Fells are mostly in Cumberland (now Cumbria) about to 2 to 3 miles south west of Glendhu. However there is a location called Glen Dhu on the south western slopes of Glendhu and in Cumberland. So where exactly did the aircraft crash?

Bill Steele, who as a small boy lived at Willowbog recalls that a small aircraft painted bright yellow crashed and was then recovered from the high ground to the south of the Lewis Burn between High Long House and Low Long House, probably around the area known as Burnt Tom. He also recalls that this occurred around about the same time as the crash of Halifax DK116. These facts would seem to suggest that this aircraft was Tiger Moth T6828. The aircraft Bill Steele describes was bright yellow, which by 1944 was the standard colour scheme for training aircraft, and it had an open cockpit. Both of these details could be included in the description of a Tiger Moth. Unfortunately Bill Steele remembers the aircraft as being relatively intact whereas the RAF accident report recalls that there had been a fire, and that the aircraft was burnt out. But a substantial part of the aircraft must have been recovered because it is recorded as being allocated to a repair depot on the 22/11/1944. So on the balance of the available information it would seem likely that Tiger Moth T6828 was the aircraft which crashed on Burnt Tom. This Burnt Tom (grid ref. NY595820) should not however be confused with another hill of the same name only about 3 ½ half miles to the south west (grid ref. 595820).

The Bewcastle Fells lie just to the west of this site. It is known that a number of aircraft, including several Hurricanes and a Beaufighter, crashed in this area during the war. The area is so isolated, desolate and sparsely populated that any recall of these of these events or indeed of an accurate location for them seems very unlikely and rather than speculate about them the stories of these aircrafts' violent ends have neither been investigated nor attempted to be told.

The Reminders

Today, nearly 60 years on, artefacts still exist which serve as reminders of these events.

Perhaps the most poignant, possibly the most permanent and certainly the most numerous of these are the graves of the unfortunate airmen who lost their lives in these tragic events. None of them now lie within the hill area of the Borders and a list of the location of these graves (where known) appears in appendix V.

Of the airfields involved in these events very few remain in use and most are only represented by a derelict "Maycrete" building or perhaps a stretch of crumbling runway. RAF Leeming, as will be related later in the "Sequels," remains in full operational use whilst Kingstown has become Carlisle Airport. Croft has been developed into a motor racing circuit whilst the site at Acklington is now a prison although much of the outfield is presently an opencast coal mine. This same opencast site has swallowed up part of Eshott but flying still takes place from the truncated remains of the runways there. These are close to the A1 trunk road and the airfield is now named Bokenfield. The majority of the flying which takes place involves micro-light aircraft.

Of the other Border airfields East Fortune is possibly the most complete. Two wartime hangers have been refurbished and now house the "Museum of Flight". This museum's collection includes some WW II artefacts, excellently laid out, and is well worth a visit. There are a number of other buildings still standing at the site, including the parachute packing building.

Up until the mid-1990s hangers and substantial sections of runway remained at Milfield but these have now disappeared as the area from which gravel extraction is taking place at the site has expanded. Some buildings of the Admin. site still survive on the eastern side of airfield. There never were many buildings at Brunton, Milfield's satellite, and now there are none at all although a substantial proportion of the runway, perimeter track and dispersals still remain.

Some flying is carried out from these remains of the runways and is mostly associated with the Borders Parachute Club. The land within the airfield site has been returned to agriculture and for the last five years a Vintage Tractor Rally has been held in the autumn on part of the runway system. A small corner on the south western side of the site is still retained by the RAF and has a radar site on it. This is controlled by RAF Boulmer which is also still an active RAF station. The runways there have been shortened and built over, but in addition to its use as a radar complex, some service flying is still carried out by the Sea King helicopters of 'A' flight,

202 Squadron. They operate in an Air-Sea rescue role.

Further south Unsworth's site is now shared by the Nissan car plant and the North East aircraft Museum having become Sunderland Airport during the 60s and 70s. Ouston continued to be used by the RAF until the late 60's when they relinquished it to the Army who renamed it Albermarle Barracks.

Charter Hall and its satellite Winfield have both retained some of their runways and a limited amount of flying by light aircraft is carried out, mostly associated with parachute jumping. For a period in the 60s and 70s Charter Hall was used as a motor racing circuit, being particularly popular with the motor cycling branch of that sport. In the late summer of 1995 Charter Hall once again became involved in military flying, albeit very briefly. This was when a RAF Hercules of the Lyneham Wing performed " touch and go" landings there and also undertook full landings followed by rapid loading and unloading of its cargo. This was believed to be in connection with a possible deployment of Hercules aircraft to relieve the besieged city of Sarajevo at the height of the Bosnian crisis.

Examples of most of the types of aircraft mentioned in this guide still exist. Some are static museum exhibits but a number are airworthy and can be seen at Air Displays around Great Britain during the summer months. Perhaps the most notable collection of static aircraft is held at the RAF Museum at Hendon and this includes German as well as Allied aircraft. The Imperial War Museum also houses a representative collection at its facility at Duxford. Flying examples of two Hawker Hurricanes, several Supermarine Spitfires, and an Avro Lancaster are maintained by the Battle of Britain Memorial Flight at RAF Coningsby in Lincolnshire. It is possible to visit and be shown around these aircraft at their home base. Such visits are highly recommended and it is often possible to witness the aircraft taking off, either on test flights or departing to take part in a display. The sight and sound of these aircraft taking to the air is evocative of a past, but dramatic era, and is well worth the long journey to see and hear. You would be unlikely to get as close to these aircraft at a display as you can at Coningsby.

Other flying and static examples of aircraft exist throughout Great Britain. Many of these aircraft, including flying examples of a Fortress (the Sally B), a Blenheim, and a Mustang, are privately owned but are accessible to the general public at local museums and flying displays. An aircraft very worthy of mention is the Halifax III which has recently been restored at the Yorkshire Air Museum, formerly RAF Elvington. Although a composite of parts from all over the world the aircraft is shown as NP—T of 158 Squadron and christened by its crew "Friday the 13th". The significance of this is that NP—T was the first Halifax to complete a hundred operational missions. The restored aircraft was rolled out for static display on Friday the 13th November 1996, an occasion marked by a fly past of Tornado F3s from RAF Leeming.

Sadly no examples, not even static, of some of the types of aircraft now exist and included in this group are the Whitley, the Beaufort, and the Master.

The Border Counties Railway was closed for use in 1956 and the Waverly route in 1969 but their trackbeds, over and under bridges, viaducts etc still remain. At the point of their meeting, Riccarton Junction, the schoolmaster's house still stands, a reminder of a small, isolated, and close knit community. A grassy bank, all that remains of the station platform, at the confluence of the two track beds is the only vestige of the

All that remains of 'Riccarton Junction.' House in the trees is the old schoolmaster's house. Puddle in foreground is where the Border Union Railway met the Waverley route. Dark line of vegetation running towards small building on left represents the position of the station platform.

once, extensive railway buildings.

At some of the crash sites pieces of wreckage still exist, and serve as a reminder of the crash and also of the lives that may have been lost. At the sites where wreckage can still be seen the amount and size of this wreckage varies considerably. A disturbing trend has occurred over the last few years with many of these pieces being removed from crash sites

92

not just here in the Borders but all over the UK. The people responsible for this desecration are usually only interested in acquisition not inquisition. Even those groups whose intention it is to put the parts on display do not escape criticism for frequently their intention never becomes reality and the parts become lost for ever, and even if it is displayed the part is out of the environment in which the event occurred. Furthermore, left at the original site, these pieces of wreckage are accessible to everyone — once removed that accessibility becomes limited. This removal of wreckage has become even more distasteful as it has now been revealed that some of the parts have been changing hands for money and that a distinct "trade" has developed.

To avoid any recurrence of such activity OS grid references will not be given in this guide for those crash sites where it is considered that there is a high-risk of the disappearance of the site because of the very small amount of material which is available for removal. However a description of the general area of the site will be given. Similarly, no grid reference will be given where the site is on private land and access to it is restricted because of other activities i.e. grouse shoots, military training, etc.

A description of the location of those pieces of wreckage known to exist and all of the crash sites now follows in the same chronological order as the crashes occurred.

Bristol Blenheim K7067

Several parts of this aircraft still exist just to the south of Cottonshope farm. Remember that access to this area is restricted as it is part of the Otterburn Range and permission should be sought from the farmer before entering his land.

Piece of Blenheim K7067 wreckage held by David Earl, author of 'Hell On High Ground,' close to Cottonshope Farm.

93

Section of Blenheim K7067 wreckage used as a culvert near Cottonshore Farm.

Armstrong Whitworth Whitley V P4952 ZA-R

What few remains that were left at this site were removed by the North Eastern Aircraft Museum some years ago. All that now remains is a shallow depression in the ground in which a very small number of small pieces of alloy can be unearthed. This is at OS grid ref. NY794822.

Armstrong Whitworth Whitley V P4957 ZA-E

One small piece of fuselage skinning still remains where the aircraft came to rest. It is located on the North-eastern end of the ridge which separates the Gelt burn from its tributary which flows down Guy's Cleugh. This is at the head of Knarsdale approximately three miles south-west of Slaggyford village. The area lies between Gilling Brigg and Guy's Middle. This is privately owned land over which there are no public footpaths and no rights of way. Furthermore, this land is used for grouse shoots but the shooting rights are not held by the farmer and so permission to reach the site is required from both the farmer and the gamekeeper and is unlikely to be given at certain times of the year. The land is owned by the farmer at Far House, about 2 miles south-west of Slaggyford.

The small dog is standing in the depression, the only relic of the site of the crash of Whitley P4952.

The only surviving piece of Whitley P4957 (ZA-E).

Hills in the background lie to the east of the South Tyne Valley.

Vickers Wellington Ic T2546 VF-A

There are no remains or even marks in the ground at the site of this crash at OS grid ref. NY839938. Up until the mid 1980s there was a gap in the field boundary wall which was made by the aircraft as it crashed. However, the wall was removed during drainage work carried out by the Ministry of Agriculture's Experimental Husbandry Farm at Redesdale. This was just to the west of the wall and some small aircraft parts were revealed during this work. It is thought that they were reburied.

Ju 88A-1 Werke Nr 7122 VB + KM

Remains of this aircraft are known to have existed until the early 1960s when the area surrounding the site was planted with trees. This site is at OS grid ref. NY537903 but local recall has no recent recollection of the wreckage being seen. A piece of the wreckage, namely a hatch cover which broke away from the aircraft before it crashed, was used at Raltonside Farm as a cover for the sheep dipper for many years, but is thought that when this dipper was demolished in the mid 1980s in order to comply with new Health and Safety Regulations this cover was bulldozed with the rest of the rubble into the footings of the new circular dipper.

Miles Master III W8694

The ruins of Redsike Farm. At one time the nearest habitation to the crash site of Master W8594. Abandoned in the early 1960's.

96

No remains of any kind. The crash site is at OS grid ref. NY625787. This grid reference is approximate and the actual impact of the aircraft could have occurred anywhere within a radius of 200 m of that point.

Hawker Hurricane Z2349

Area now afforested. No remains have ever been known to exist. Site is at OS grid ref. NY545977.

Hawker Hurricane Z3150 VT-V

Wreckage of Hurricane Z3150 VT-V on Peel Fell. Propellor reduction gear and hub are prominent. Photo:- J. Corbett.

Several pieces of wreckage still exist at this site including the propeller reduction gear. Site is at OS grid ref. NY620997 (approx. - accurate to within 100 metres).

Hawker Hurricane N2428

Area now afforested. No remains have ever been known to exist. Approx. site of crash OS grid ref. NT 535014 (probably accurate to within the 200 metres).

B-17E Fortress IIA FK204 NR-N

No wreckage thought to exist. Accurate OS grid ref. for site is difficult to give as wreckage was scattered for 600 metres but is in the area of NU 010229.

Supermarine Spitfire I R7202

Some small remains of this aircraft are known to exist but have not been seen for some years as the heather has become much more rank. The site is on private land but is close to the Border County Ride where it exits Harwood Forest on Darden Rigg.

North American Mustang I AG 617

Robert Anderson standing beside the few relics of Mustang AG617 at its crash site.

A substantial part of this aircraft is thought to remain below the peat. However the area is so wet that any attempts at recovery are impossible. Nevertheless unsuccessful efforts have been made and small pieces of aluminium now lie on the surface at the site as a result of these probings. The site is located at OS grid ref. NY832904. The area surrounding the site is almost featureless and this makes location of the site difficult.

Bristol Beaufort I DX118

No remains of any kind known to exist. The site of crash is at OS grid ref. NT 795093. As there are no remains this position of the crash site must be regarded as approximate but is probably accurate to within 100 metres.

De Havilland Tiger Moth N9462

The whole of the wreckage of this aircraft was removed not long after the crash occurred. The site of the crash is at OS grid ref. NY 615829. Once again this position is approximate but is probably accurate to within 200 metres.

Vickers Wellington Ic X3171

Local enthusiasts have searched for pieces of this aircraft with metal detectors but without success. A very approximate position for the crash is at OS grid ref. NY778922 but it should be stressed that this could be very inaccurate indeed, by possibly as much as 500 metres.

German aircraft crashed 25/03/1943

No remains known to exist at sites.

Avro Lancaster II DS 650 ND-P

Most of the wreckage of the aircraft was removed from the hillside and dumped at the point where the road to Cottonshope meets the A68. It lay there for several years but was then removed. Small pieces of perspex and solidified molten aluminium were found when the trees were felled in the early 1970s at OS grid ref. NT 766033. A large piece of tail assembly including part of the fin structure lay just to the South of Blakehopeburnhaugh Farm for many years but is believed to have been buried under a newly made forest track in the 1960s. A propeller blade

The grave of J. Simms, bomb aimer of Lancaster DS 650, in Stonefall Cemetery, Harrogate.

from this aircraft was reported to have lain close to the Forest Drive to Kielder but has now disappeared.

Handley Page Halifax II JP190

An unidentifiable piece of the wreckage of Halifax JP190 in Craik Forest.

100

A small piece of the wreckage of Hallifax JP190. The number cast into it identifies it as part of the engine nacelle/undercarriage structure.

A small amount of wreckage from this aircraft remains at crash site which is now afforested. These remains lie about 300 metres south of the forest track which runs west from Wolfcleuchhead and about 700 metres west of the house there. A small wooden cross has been set amongst the wreckage which is well hidden by the trees. Please remember that this land is owned by Forest Enterprise and although an Outdoor Activity Centre exists at Craik it would only be common courtesy to let Forest Enterprise know of your intention to visit the site.

Handley Page Halifax V DK 116

A large amount of wreckage remains at this site. The O S. grid ref. is NY 580866. The area surrounding the site is completely planted with trees and so there are no features by which to navigate and fire breaks must be used to reach the crash site. A forest track runs alongside the Lewis Burn and at a point OS grid ref. NY584857 an obviously trodden path disappears north westwards into the trees. The crash site can be reached by following the trodden path along the firebreaks. This is not always obvious and care should be taken. The site has clearly been dug over by "wreckology" groups and it is known that one of Merlin engines, thought to be the starboard outer, was pulled from the peat and removed

101

Large part of undercarriage of Halifax DK116 lying in Kielder Forest.

Large amount of wreckage of Hallifax DK116 in Kielder Forest.

102

about 25 years ago when the trees were still quite small. The easiest way to reach the site is to drive along the forest track which follows the Lewis Burn until the point mentioned above is reached. This track is passable by 2-wd drive vehicles but care should be exercised. You should obtain permission to use this track from Forest Enterprise and inform them of your intention to visit the site. A pass will then be issued. For those with more time and energy it is possible to make the whole journey on foot. Visits to this site during July, August and early September are not recommended due to the large "midgy" population which then stands guard over the wreckage, and can be very irritating indeed.

A more modern reminder of a much more recent event is the small German cross next to the road at Stannersburn which commemorates the crew of a Luftwaffe Tornado which crashed nearby.

It is worthwhile remembering that many farmers and landowners are not very enthusiastic about metal detectors being used over their land, as it gives rise to serious legal problems if anything of value, other than pieces of aircraft wreckage, is detected on that land.

 **The grave of P/O J.C. Lees, pilot of Halifax MZ908, in Stonefall Cemetary, Harrogate.**

The Sequels

In the time that has elapsed since these events took place a number of connected episodes have occurred including some of the people and places involved in those original incidents.

By July 1941 Hewitt Idwal Evans, the pilot of Blenheim K 7067, had attained the rank of Acting Wing Commander. He was Commanding Officer of 105 Squadron and was still flying Blenheims, albeit the longer nosed Mk IV version. On 04/07/1941, the squadron was ordered to make a daylight attack on a pinpoint target in the German dockyard town of Bremen. This attack had to be carried out a very low altitude and as it was a daylight raid the defences were alerted and waiting. For his valour and leadership in pressing home his attack Wing Commander Edwards was awarded the Victoria Cross. This was added to the Distinguished Flying Cross he had already been awarded for a similar low-level attack against shipping off the Dutch coast in June. He went on to be promoted to higher rank and assumed more commander responsibility. After the war he became Governor General of Western Australia.

Of the five men who parachuted to safety from Whitley P4952 (ZA-R) of 10 Squadron on 15/10/1940, three were members of the crew of Whitley T4230,(also ZA-R) when it took off for operation against an oil plant at Merburg on 13/11/1940. These were S/L K.F. Ferguson, Sgt Rogers and Sgt Fraser. On this occasion, however, S/L Ferguson's luck seemed to have finally run out and the aircraft failed to return to base. No trace of it was ever found. The crew were all assumed to have died.

Sgt. Mark Niman, one of the two remaining members of the crew of P4952, went on to complete a "tour" of missions. Most of his operational missions were flown with a crew captained by Sgt. Hickling but in early May 1941 his last two operational missions with 10 Squadron were flown with a crew captained by a W/C Bennett, but not he who was later to achieve fame as the originator and leader of Bomber Command's Pathfinders. Having completed his operational "tour" Sgt Niman became an instructor for a short time before being transferred to the Overseas Aircraft Delivery Flight. On 06/07/1941 Sgt Niman was part of a crew detailed to deliver a Bristol Bombay, L5837, from Redruth, in Cornwall to 216 Squadron based at Heliopolis. On this occasion Sgt Niman was the W/Op. The aircraft had been fitted with extra inboard fuel tanks in order to extend its range to be capable of reaching Gibraltar. The fuel in these tanks had to be hand pumped into the normal fuel tanks in the wings. Some time into the flight whilst making a routine D/F radio check Sgt

Niman noticed a stream of petrol flowing off the trailing edge of the wings. On investigation it was found that the pumping of the fuel from the inboard tanks had been over enthusiastic and had over filled the normal wing tanks. A not inconsiderable amount of fuel had disappeared into the ocean below. A quick calculation showed that insufficient fuel now remained for the aircraft to reach Gibraltar and the decision was made by the pilot and captain, P/O J. Turner to ditch in the sea once the fuel was exhausted. Sgt Niman sent an S.O.S. and an air sea rescue launch was sent from Gibraltar to rendezvous with the aircraft. P/O Turner made excellent landing on the sea, especially considering that the Bombay was a fixed undercarriage aircraft, and the aircraft stayed afloat because of the extra buoyancy given to it by all the empty fuel tanks. An attempt was made by the air sea rescue launch to take the aircraft in tow but this failed when the aircraft engines, to which the tow hawser had been attached, were pulled off the wings and fell into the sea. Sgt Niman and the rest of a crew were safely delivered to "The Rock" where they enjoyed a few days rest before returning to England to start the process all over again.

From May 1943 to February 1944 Sgt Niman was once again flying operationally, this time as a W/Op in anti-submarine Catalina flying boats of 259 Squadron and 209 Squadron based at various stations in the Western Indian Ocean area. He seems to have flown most of his missions in aircraft 'B' of 259 Squadron, FP247, and also aircraft 'A', FP133.

Mark Niman became operational again in February 1945 when he became a "special duties operator" with 192 Squadron. This Squadron operated Halifax III's as part of 100 Group. This group provided the aircraft equipped with electronic counter measures to protect Bomber Command's aircraft against detection. Its aircraft carried a full bomb load and flew in the main stream of "ordinary" bombers during a raid. They did, however, have extra electronic equipment on board and this could either interfere with the enemy radar, making detection less likely, or send out transmissions which confused the Germans. This equipment was complex and needed an extra crew member to operate it. This was the "special duties operator". Because of the electronic "emissions" produced by these aircraft they made themselves easier to detect and squadrons operating within 100 Group had much higher than average loss rates because of this. By the end of the war Mark Niman had flown 10 missions with this Squadron, had been raised to the rank of Flight Lieutenant, and also been awarded the Distinguished Flying Medal. He had also completed nearly 800 hours of flying.

Sgt George Dove flew no more missions with 10 Squadron after the crash of P4957 on 30/10/1940. He had, after all, flown one additional mission anyway. He was transferred to RAF Kinloss in Northern Scotland where he became an instructor at the OTU based there. However by early 1943 he was flying operationally again, but this time as a mid upper gunner in the Lancasters of 101 Squadron based at Holme-on-Spalding Moor, Yorkshire.

On the night of 13 - 14/02/1943 F/Sgt Dove was a member of the crew of Lancaster ED377 coded SR-X which took part in a mission against Milan in Northern Italy. The aircraft was captained by Sgt Ivan Hazard and reached Milan without difficulty. Once there it's lethal load was dropped on the city below and the aircraft turned for home. Not long after this SR-X was attacked by a night fighter. Unfortunately not all of SR-X's bomb load had left the aircraft and four 30 lb phosphorus bombs which had "hung up" were ignited by the night fighter's machine gun fire. These bombs were directly beneath F/ Sgt Dove's turret. The rear gunner, though wounded, managed to get in a burst of fire against the enemy fighter and set its engine on fire. Despite the fact that the mid upper turret was enveloped in flames and that his hand and face were already burnt F/Sgt Dove also got in another burst of fire and saw the enemy fighter fall away to its destruction. But now the Lancaster had its own problems, with one engine on fire, a fuel tank punctured and losing fuel rapidly, and perhaps most seriously an inferno in which ammunition was exploding in the fuselage. Regardless of his own injuries F/Sgt Dove climbed from his turret into the flames, and although now isolated from his oxygen supply, made his way back through this conflagration in order to free the rear gunner who was now bleeding profusely. Sgt Hazard then ordered the crew to be prepared to abandon the aircraft but was told that the rear gunner was too seriously injured to bale out. He put the bomber into a steep dive and after having dropped from 17,000 feet to 6000 feet, the high speed of the dive had extinguished the fire with some help from the crew who had been working overtime with fire extinguishers. Rather then crash in enemy territory Sgt Hazard elected to try and make it back to Britain. The battered Lancaster, now flying on three engines, managed to claw its way over the Alps and avoiding anti-aircraft gun sites in France finally crossed the English Channel. Unknown to the crew both they and the aircraft had already been posted as missing at Holme-on-Spalding Moor. With some difficulty, because of low cloud and a lack of hydraulics to operate the undercarriage, SR-X finally touched down at RAF Tangmere. It was not until the aircraft had landed that the severity and extent of George Dove's injuries and burns were finally revealed. While the rest of the crew were given two weeks survivors leave F/Sgt Dove was sent to the special burns unit at East Grinstead hospital set up by the surgeon Archibald McIndoe. This was where pioneering work in plastic surgery was carried out on injured airmen, in particular those suffering from the

106

horrific burns caused by aircraft fires. Eventually George Dove's injuries were healed and he returned to duty. But higher authority insisted that he had had enough of operational flying and he spent the rest of the war as an instructor, finally reaching the rank of Flying Officer.

George Dove's actions in the air above Milan that night brought a recommendation from his squadron c/o, that he be awarded the Victoria Cross. In the eventuality he was awarded the Conspicuous Gallantry Medal, to add to his Distinguished Flying Medal, and became one of only a small handful of men to be given both honours.

Lancaster ED377 (SR- X) was recorded by its manufacturers A.V.Roe Ltd, as being the most severely damaged aircraft of its type returned to them for repair up to that date.

Sadly, George Dove was the only member of the crew of Whitley P4957 which crashed on 30 /10 /1940 to survive the war. Three of the other members of the crew died as a result of being shot down on separate operational flights whilst Sgt Ottway had the misfortune to be a passenger in a Halifax returning from the Middle East which was shot down over the Bay of Biscay.

In the late 1980s a former member of 43 Squadron ground crew finally went to site of the crash of Hurricane Z3150 to investigate if anything remained there. Jim Beedle's quest had been a long time ambition and not only had he been involved in aircraft archaeology for a considerable length of time but was also involved in the Tangmere Museum. The Tangmere Museum had come into being to preserve those artefacts which had any association with RAF Tangmere, one of the Battle of Britain airfields. This included those items with connections to 43 Squadron which had spent a considerable length of time stationed at Tangmere, especially during the period of the Battle of Britain. Jim Beedle's interest in the crash site was made even greater because he had actually worked on Z3150 and had known P/O "Joe" Mehta quite well.

Armed with such records of the event as he could find and with some local help Jim found the crash site in the summer of 1987. With the help of other enthusiasts he dug down and discovered large parts of the air frame, including wing sections and parts of the tail assembly embedded in the peat. Armour plate, cockpit components, the propeller, hub and engine carburettor were also found and such items of that could be were manhandled down Peel Fell and taken to be preserved at the Tangmere Museum. Sadly, this was to be Jim Beedle's last project for he died following a short illness only months after his successful hunt for Z3150.

The injured man that Adam Steele had found on the night of 15/10/1944 was Sgt J. Mahoney. Not only did Adam Steele find the man but he also found his parachute. Recognising that it was probably of some value, but unable to retrieve it that night, he carefully put it behind some rocks to be collected at a later date. Once the furore of the crash had died down Adam collected the parachute and Bill Steele, Adam's son remembers that not only did the silk provide dresses for his sisters for many years but the chords tied up the joints of ham and pork from the home killed pigs for a similar length of time.

The three young Anderson boys from High Cranecleugh all still live and farm in the area. By some amazing coincidence Brian now farms at Brieredge where Whitley P4952 crashed; Hew (Matthew) farms at Blakehope where Wellington T2546 came to grief and Robert lives at Blakehopeburnhaugh where part of the tail section of Lancaster DS650 was discovered. Incidentally Blakehopeburnhaugh is the longest single place name in England.

All the Anderson brothers remember that for a short time towards the end of the war, and perhaps for a similar time after the war, Sgt Dicken's wife visited their mother and father together with her son, Derek. It is known that Sgt Dicken survived the war and it seems strange that he did not return to visit the Andersons along with his wife.

A vast tract of Upper Redesdale and the catchment area of Upper North Tynedale had been sold to the Forestry Commission in the early 1930s. In 1933 the first plantings were made and these progressed steadily until the start of World War II when they came to a halt. The farms of High Cranecleugh and Otterstone Lea were already sold to the Forest Commission when the crashes of Tiger Moth N 9462 and Halifax the DK116 occurred on them. High Cranecleugh in fact, had all the stock removed shortly after the incident and planting restarted there the next year. These trees have reached maturity and already been felled and the area has been planted again. High Cranecleugh has been renamed Broomy Lynn whilst Low Cranecleugh is now a holiday and recreational centre, specialising in providing facilities for the disabled.

The wreckage of Halifax DK116 was in such a remote place that no attempt was ever made to remove it. It was, however, covered with a net in order to camouflage it, in the hope that this would prevent overflying aircraft from seeing it and reporting it as a new crash site. This seems to have been successful. The whole area surrounding it was planted with trees in the early mid 1950s and this timber is now reaching maturity.

In addition to the afforestation a large amount of land was also lost when the the River North Tyne was dammed near Falstone to form a reservoir known as Kielder Water. This is reputed to be the largest man made lake in Europe, a claim disputed by the operators and "fans" of Rutland Water.

In the early 1990 an ATC Squadron from Edinburgh took an interest in the crash of Halifax JP190. Eventually their interest resulted in the erection and dedication of a memorial plaque at the Forest Amenity Centre at Craik. It is known that some of the families of those who lost their lives attended this dedication ceremony. Unfortunately the actual details of this event are not recorded accurately. Also unfortunately the small memorial plaque has had to be temporarily removed as the weather is having dire effects on whatever material it is made from but plans are in hand to reinstate it. At around the same time a simple wooden cross was placed at the actual site of the crash and still stands at the present time (August 1998).

Their have been several military aircraft crashes in this area since the war. Although not within the remit of this guide they do warrant a mention in that they serve to emphasise the dangers of low flying in this hilly area.

One of the more notable of these was the crash of a BAe Jaguar at Craik Cross in the early 1980s only a short distance from the crash site of Halifax JP190.

Several modern aircraft are known to have crashed on the Otterburn ranges including a Harrier flown by an American pilot on secondment to the RAF. In 1975 a General Dynamics F111 crashed near Selkirk, with the loss of both its USAF crew. Ironically the Luffwaffe has also suffered further losses. This was when, on 24/10/1985 a Tornado of JGD32 on a low flying NATO exercise clipped the tips of some of the Kielder Forest trees, lost control and subsequently crashed on a wooded hill top at Stannersburn. The crew of Hans-Joachim Schumpf and Holge Zacharias were unfortunately killed instantly. By almost unbelievable coincidence one of, if not, the first people at the scene of the crash was Robert Anderson who purely by chance happened to be doing some work for the Forestry Commission close to the scene of the accident.

RAF Leeming has remained in use and has developed into one of the RAF's busiest stations with a considerable amount of its resources committed to NATO involvement.

It was also the scene of only the second reunion of George Dove and Mark Niman since those heady but dark days with 10 Squadron in the autumn of 1940. This took place in August 1998, the two men having previously remet at the former RAF Elvington site, now the Yorkshire Air Museum, in 1994. But now the men had met at the base from which they had both taken off on flights which had ended in high drama.

In March 1999 the two men met again this time in the C/O's

The memorial to the crew of the Luftwaffe Tornado which crashed at Stannersburn in October, 1985.

Office at RAF Leeming. The C/O Grp. Capt. J.A. Cliffe, was presented with memorabilia of 10 Squadron's service at Leeming in 1940 by the two veteran airmen.

Finally in May 1999 Mark Niman visited Northumberland. A keen member of the RAF Association, he stayed at that organisation's home at Rothbury. Whilst there he was visited by Tommy Thompson who regaled him with stories of the wrecked aircraft.

And then he visited the final resting place of Whitley P4952. At the site he was lucky enough to find a small piece of wreckage. Little had he thought of that when he entered the aircraft on that fateful night in October 1940 that he would come face to face with a part of it 59 years later.

George Dove and Mark Niman reunited at Leeming,
August 1998, in front of a Tornado F3 (ZE 201). A 'little'
different to the Whitleys of 58 years previously!
Photo:- RAF Leeming.

The Conclusions

The sky above the Border hills is still regularly used by modern military aircraft. Very few of them have come to any harm at all unlike their forebears of 50 years ago. So what were the chief causes of those wartime accidents, and were there any common factors which may have contributed to them? And if there were what has now prevented these same factors causing similar accidents at the present time?

None of the accidents involving single engined or single seat aircraft happened as the result of a mechanical defect. But the reports about all of them always mention flying in cloud, poor visibility and inclement weather. Most of the pilots of these aircraft were relatively inexperienced, sometimes very inexperienced, and in the case of nearly every incident the words "disorientated" or "lost" are used. It would seem then that a major cause of crashes for this group of aircraft was inexperience, this resulting in the inability to cope with poor visibility or being "lost" due to that same lack of visibility.

However, the reasons are not nearly so clear-cut for the multi-engined bomber aircraft. The crews of the two Whitleys and the Wellington which crashed in the Autumn of 1940 were reasonably well experienced as borne out by the fact that they had already flown several operational missions. None of these three aircraft was suffering from any mechanical problems and their crashes can all be attributed to the fact that they did not know, with any precision, exactly where they were. The fact that the Wellington's radio equipment was unserviceable did not directly cause its crash, rather more that the lack of a radio contributed to the aircraft being lost. Similarly, lack of fuel was the factor which ultimately led to the crash of Whitley P4952 but this shortage of fuel was itself caused by the aircraft being unable to pinpoint its position. These early Bomber Command missions were pioneering military aviation. The force of bombers, and it was not large, was sent out in small fragmented groups, each group being given a separate target to attack. It is therefore not surprising that little damage was done by these early raids and also that aircraft became lost, because if larger numbers had been sent then these aircraft would have had many other aircraft flying alongside them perhaps leading each other home. Incidentally these early raids of Bomber Command attract little comment nowadays and it is not widely known that the bombing campaign was up and running even as the Battle of Britain was being waged.

Mechanical failure of some kind played a part in many of the later crashes of these larger aircraft. The Beaufort suffered engine failure and this was the sole cause of its crash.

112

If the stories of ground eye witnesses are taken into account it would seem that all the Halifaxes involved had suffered some kind of mechanical failure. But in the case of JP190 the subsequent RAF report does not corroborate the eye witnesses evidence of the aircraft being on fire. This is also true of Lancaster DS650. In the case of these two aircraft the evidence of the ground eye witnesses must be treated with a certain degree of caution. There is a strong likelihood that what they may have seen was the glare produced by the exhaust systems of the engines. Certainly it is on record that the Merlin 22 installation of the Halifax produced a large amount of glare at night and several experimental schemes were tried out in an attempt to reduce it, all without too much success. Similarly, the Hercules XVI of the Lancaster also had a glare problem, the exhaust collector ring, which formed the nose of the engine nacelle glowed like a gas ring at night. Attempts were also made to reduce this, the only partially successful one being the application of a special gold paint. Given the doubt concerning the existence of an engine fire in the case of both Halifax JP190 and Lancaster DS650 then another factor may have contributed to the crashes of these two aircraft. This could most probably have been the inexperience of the pilots.With regard to Halifax JP190 he probably became aware of high ground ahead of him, pulled up the aircraft's nose in an attempt to avoid it and inadvertently stalled the aircraft. It is also possible that pilot inexperience contributed to the loss of control of Lancaster DS650. But the possibility of a structural failure cannot be ruled out. Some time after the accident occurred it was discovered that in certain critical flight conditions the fabric covering of the tailplane control surfaces could balloon out and then rip off, giving rise to just the kind of power dive described by the eye witness. But as this phenomenon had not been discovered at the time of the accident then it was not even taken into consideration as being a likely cause of the crash leaving loss of control by the pilot as the sole explanation.

The crash of Wellington X3171 on Blackburn Fell, was probably also due to some kind of pilot error most likely to have been the result of inexperience.

Being lost due to various factors such as bad visibility caused by inclement weather, poor or unserviceable navigational and radio equipment, or a combination of these factors would seem to have been the most common cause of these accidents. Mechanical problems, however, were also responsible for a significant number of these crashes, sometimes, as in the case of Fortress FK204, in conjunction with poor weather. Lack of pilot experience, was not often the sole cause of a crash, but acted in conjunction with the other factors on numerous occasions.

But were the Border Hills in anyway implicated in any of these events? The answer to that question is a resounding "yes". Certainly for those aircraft that were lost, the avoidance of a feature of which it was a unaware, directly in its path, was patently not possible and the resulting crash almost inevitable. However, the high ground had no part to play in those accidents which were a result of some mechanical defect or solely due to pilot inexperience. No matter what terrain lay beneath those aircraft these events would still have occurred. It is possible to argue that in the case of Halifax DK116 that if the aircraft had not been flying over high ground then it is just possible that the whole crew may have been able to parachute to safety. But even if one accepts that reasoning it is only the result of the crash which was affected by the hills and not the cause of it.

The design, construction and equipment of modern military aircraft has to a large extent eliminated those factors which have been shown to have been the cause of the wartime crashes. For instance it is almost impossible for a modern aircraft, either military or civil, to be lost due to the navigational systems now incorporated in their designs. The inertial navigational systems used in all military aircraft mean that the aircraft knows it's exact position at all times. This system is, in effect, a very modern, and automated version of the old "Dead Reckoning" method of navigation.

The difference is that now changes in speed, direction and altitude are constantly measured by extremely sensitive gyroscopes, and these changes fed into a computer which instantaneously calculates the new course and hence new position(s). Even in the event of an aircraft not being aware of its exact position sophisticated systems are in place either to warn the pilot of high ground beneath or ahead of his aircraft or even to automatically manoeuvre the aircraft out of danger. Among these devices are radio altimeters, ground proximity radar and most sophisticated of all Terrain Following radar (TFR). TFR allows low flying fast jets to follow the ground beneath them at a precise and very low altitude, automatically with little input from the pilot. A radar beam projected ahead and downwards from the aircraft maps out the topography of the land ahead and then via a computer linked to the aircraft controls maintains the aircraft at the pre-set height above that terrain. Very recently a less sophisticated version of this device has been developed for civilian aircraft.

Although not impossible mechanical defects in modern aircraft are very rare. Several factors have influenced this change from the situation which existed during WW II. Modern aircraft go through a much more thorough testing and development programme than their forebears and this is in some way due to the fact that the same pressures do not exist to get a new type into production. They are therefore less likely to have

114

any in-built faults. Jets engines are inherently more reliable than piston engines as they have far fewer moving parts, and these parts are all rotating and not, as in the case of a piston engines, reciprocating and rotating. Electrical and electronic equipment is also much more reliable as modern systems employ such techniques as solid state components and printed circuits.

And finally modern aircrew are, with great respect to those who flew in WWII, much more experienced and trained to an extremely high calibre before they are allowed to fly operationally. Once again this is due to the absence of a conflict reducing the pressure to replace aircrew, resulting in a greater amount of available time to train them. The selection pressure on initial appointment of aircrew is also much less, resulting in only the very best of candidates reaching operational flying status.

Thus it can be seen that the Border Hills no longer pose the same threat that they once did to military aircraft. And even on those occasions when the possibility of an incident occurs the awesome performance of modern supersonic jets often means that it can be avoided by simply "blasting" away from it.

The situation with regard to civil aircraft is not quite so risk free especially when taking light aircraft into consideration. It is acknowledged by the various bodies who administer aviation legislation that "terrain related incidents" are still the most frequent cause of accidents involving civilian light aircraft, with the majority of occurring on or near high ground. Mercifully, though, even these are a very uncommon occurrence.

The Border Hills are part of the RAF's Northern LLOTA (low level over land training area) and low flying military aircraft are still frequent visitors to the region but the same factors which once caused such problems with their resultant dramatic stories are now used to advantage. Rather than avoid them the Tornados, Harriers and Jaguars manoeuvre as close to them and among them as possible in an attempt to conceal themselves from the all seeing eye of all types of radar and electronic detection equipment. For these modern aircraft the hills are definitely not a "Border Too High".

Appendices

Appendix I

Operational flights of Armstrong Whitworth Whitley V P4952 (ZA-R)

All with 10 Squadron

Date	Captain	Target
1.12-13/05/1940	W/CStaton	Troop concentrations N.France
2. 17-18/05/1940	""	Bremen (oil plant)
3. 27-28/05/1940	P/O Warren	Neuss
4. 11-12/06/1940	W/C Staton	Turin
5. 12-13/07/1940	F/O Prior	Kiel (bombs not dropped)
6. 13-14/07/1940	""	Monheim (Aluminium factory)
7. 20-21/07/1940	""	Wenzendorf
8. 22-23/07/1940	""	Bremen
9. 05-06/08/1940	""	Wiemar
10. 13-14/08/1940	""	Turin
11. 16-17/08/1940	""	Zena
12. 18-19/08/1940	""	Rheinfelden
13. 24-25/08/1940	S/L Ferguson	Milan
14. 26-27/08/1940	Sgt. Towell	Milan (did not complete mission-landed Harwell)
15. 08-09/09/1940	F/O Prior	Ostend
16. 11-12/09/1940	""	Bremen
17. 14-15/09/1940	""	Antwerp
18.17-18/09/1940	""	Battleship "Bismark" at Hamburg.
19. 22-23/09/1940	""	Lauta (Aluminum factory)
20. 14-15/10/1940	SL Ferguson	Stettin

Previous operational flights by crew of above aircraft on 14-15/10/1940

Date	Aircraft	Target
1. 24-25/08/1940	P4952	Milan
2. 14-15/09/1940	P4966	Antwerp
3. 20-21/09/1940	T4176	Hamm
4. 22-23/09/1940	P5018	Lauta
5.30/09-01/10/1940	T4176	B.M.W.factory, Berlin

116

6. 07-08/10/1940   ""   Le Havre
7. 14-15/10/1940   P4952   Stettin

Crew as described in narrative

Appendix II

Operational flights of Armstrong- Whitworth V P4957(ZA-E) The aircraft
was first delivered to 10 Squadron at 1345 on 08/05/1940 together with
Whitley Vs P4961, P4962,P4963, P494 and P4965. All operational flights
with 10 Squadron.

Date	Captain	Target
15-16/05/1940	S/L Hanafin	Dinant
17-18/05/1940	""	Bremen (a/c crashed on take off-u/c retracted too early)
08-09/06/1940	""	Essen (aborted – front turret oil leak)
09-10/06/1940	""	Libramont
11-12/06/1940	""	Turin (via Guernsey – aborted after a/c struck by lightning).
13-14/06/1940	F/Sgt Witt	Chateau Thiery
14-15/06/1940	""	""
18-19/06/1940	F/O ffrench-Mullen	Schwerte
27-28/061940	F/O Henry	Duisburg
02-03/07/1940	S/L Hanafin	Hamm
20-21/07/1940	""	Wenzendorf
22-23/07/1940	F/O Nixon	Bremen
24-25/07/1940	F/O Henry	Shipping at Hamburg
02-03/08/1940	S/L Hanafin	Osnabruck (aborted-engine overheating –wireless U/S)
18-19/08/1940	F/O Henry	Rheinfelden
24-25/08/1940	S/L Hanafin	Milan (aborted after 2 hrs.-engine control problem)
26-27/08/1940	P/O Cairns	Milan
06-07//09/1940	""	Berlin
08-09/09/1940	S/L Hanafin	Ostend
11-12/09/1940	""	Bremen
14-15/09/1940	P/O Landale	Antwerp
17-18/09/1940	""	Bismark at Hamburg (aborted)

117

20-21/09/1940	Sgt Snell	Ehrang (a/c damaged
		byAA fire)
24-25/09/1940	S/L Sawyer	Berlin
27-28/09/140	""	Cherbourg
30/09-01/10/1940	P/O Peers	Le Havre
	(aborted –starboard engine failure –landed Abingdon)
10-11/10/1940	""	Cologne
14-15/10/1940	""	Le Havre
24-25/10/1940	""	Hamburg
27/-28/10/1940	""	Lorient
		(but bombed Cherbourgh)
29/30/1940	""	Wilhelmshaven

Previous operational flights by crew of P4957 on 29-30/10/1940

Date	Aircraft	Target
30/09 – 01/10/1940	P4957	Le Havre (see a/c use)
07-08/10/1940	P5055	Docks at Amsterdam
10-11/10/1940	P4957	Colgne
14-15/10/1940	P4957	Le Havre
19-20/10/1940	T4157	Osnabruck -
		marshalling yards
24-25/10/1940	P4957	Hamburg – docklands
27-28/10/1940	P4957	Lorient (see a/c use)

Crew as described in narrative.

Appendix III

Operational flights of Vickers Wellington Ic T2546
All with 99 Squadron

Date	Captain	Target
25-26/09/1940	S/L Black	Calais
28-29/09/1940	F/L Harvey	Hanau Aluminium
factory (A/c failed to find target and returned to base with bombs)
13-14/10/1940	S/L Black	Gelsenkirchen
23-24/10/1940	P/O Rothwel	Emden – docks
26-26/10/1940	S/L Black	Bremen docks
29-30/10/1940	F/L Harvey	Berlin

Previous Operational flights by crew of above aircraft on 29-30/1940

Date	Aircraft	Target
28-29/09/1940	T2546 VF-A	Hanau (see a/c flights)
1-2/10/1940	T2739 VF-V	Gelsenkirchen
7-8/10/1940	T2739 VF-V	Boulogne
9-10/10/1940	T2739 VF-V	Grevenbroich
13-14/10/1940	T2739 VF-V	Bismark at Kiel
		(actually bombed Flushing)
15-16/10/1940	T2739 VF-V	Scharnhorst at Kiel
29-30/10/1940	T2546 VF-A	Berlin

Crew as in narrative except regular rear gunner appears to have been Sgt Parker on all but last flight.

Appendix IV

Flights by North American mustang AG617. From Clifton unless otherwise stated

Date	Pilot	Purpose and Time
10/02/1943	P/O E.A Haigh	Formation Flying
11/02/1943	P/O K.M. Frost	Formation Flying 1030-1130
" " "	P/O K.M. Frost	Cloud and instr. Flying 1510-1625
12/02/1943	P/O Hindmarsh	D/F Practice 1000-1145
14/02/1943	Sgt. N. S. Cooper	Low level X-country 1100-1300
15/02/1943	" " " "	Low level X-country 1035-1205
16/02/1943	" " " "	Tactical Recon. 1045-1145
" " "	" " " "	Tactical Recon. + Photo 1410-1440
" " "	" " " "	Tactical Recon. + Photo 1515-1610
17/10/1943	" " " "	Air test 1700-1730
18/02/1943	" " " "	X – Country 1040-1200
" " "	" " " "	Tact Recon. 1420-1605
" " "	P/O Fisher	" " 1420-1605
" " "	" " " "	Clifton to East Moor 1730-1740

" " "   " " " "   Night flying from East Moor
1830-2015

19/02/1943   " " " "   East Moor to Edinburgh
1015-

Flights by P/O J. Fisher with 4 Squadron

Date	Aircraft	Purpose and Time
27/11/1942	Mustang (AG347)	Tact Recon and low flying 13-55-1440
" " "	" " " "	Aerobatics 1540-1645
30/11/1942	" " " "	Formation flying 1055-1220
01/12/1942	Tigermoth (T7804)	X-country and instrument flying with P/O Hindmarch 1435-1600
03/12/1942	Mustang (AG647)	Aerobatics 1425-1540
07/12/1942	"" (AP165)	Andover to Clifton 1415-1555
08/12/1942	"" (AG647)	To Church Fenton 1000-1100
" " "	" " " "	Return to Clifton 1345-1400
22/12/1942	" " " "	Formation flying 1400-130
29/12/1942	" " " "	Low level x-country 1030-1245
13/01/1943	" " " (AG541)	Low level x-country to Wisbech (aborted due to W/T failure)
" " "	" " " "	Successful completion of above 1040-1250
14/01/1943	" " " "	Formation flying 1300-1410
15/01/1943	" " " (AG519)	Low level attack on airfield 1140-1230
25/01/1943	" " " (AG631)	Low level X-country 1000-1145
26/01/1943	" " " (AG588)	Formation attack practice 1430-1650
29/01/1943	" " " (AG631)	York to East Moor 1700-1715
" " "	" " " "	Night Flying 1800-1840
" " "	" " " "	Tact Recon 1055-1155
18/02/1943	Details as per aircraft Mustang AG617 flights.	

120

Appendix V

Location of graves of those airmen who lost their lives.

These are recorded in chronological order and are grouped as crews where that is applicable. Where airmen are listed as crews they appear in surname alphabetical order.

Allied

Name and Rank	Date	Aircraft
		Location of Grave
P/O E.S.I.Hallows	30/09/1940	WellingtonT2456
		WillesdenJewish Cemetery
Sgt G.F. Hillie	29/09/1941	Master W8594
		Carlisle (Dalston Road) Cemetery
Sgt. J. Manby	13/10/1941	Hurricane Z2349
Cremated –remembered on memorial panel Manchester Crematorium		
P/O Hukm Chand Mehta	03/11/1941	Hurricane Z3150
		Cremated
Sgt D. Fraser	12/06/1942	Hurricane N2428
		Carlisle (Dalston Rd.) Cemetery
P/O J. Fisher	19/02/1943	Mustang AG617
		Edinburgh (Seafield)Cemetery
F.O. W.B. Milton	24/02/1943	Beaufort DX118
		Cremated – ashes returned to USA
Sgt A.W. Stevenson	01/03/1943	Tiger Moth N9462
		Manor Park Cemetery, Essex

Crew of Wellington X3171

Sgt D.L. Barley	01/03/1943	
		St Marylebone Cemetery, London
Sgt D.R. Bending	01/03/1943	
		Tainton (St Mary's) Cemetery
P/O J. Donnelly	01/03/1943	
		Kilwinning Cemetery, Ayrshire
Sgt W. S. Gibson	01/03/1943	
		Stamfordham (St Mary) Churchyard Northumberland
Sgt G. Marshall	01/03/1943	
		Trimdon Grange Cemetery, Durham
P/O T. Winstanley	01/03/1943	
		Stretford Cemetery, Lancashire

Crew of Lancaster DS650

Sgt. Robert Bell   03/03/1944
                          Newcastle upon Tyne

P/O R.G. Calder   03/03/1944
                          Edinburgh (Morningside) Cemetery

F/Sgt R.W. Campbell 03/03/1944
                          Stonefall Cemetery, Harrogate

Sgt R.C. Gibbs   03/03/1944
                          Bristol

W.O.2. F. J. Leech   03/03/1944
                          Stonefall Cemetery, Harrogate

Sgt J. Simms   03/03/1944
                          Stonefall Cemetery, Harrogate

Sgt J Speight   03/03/1944
                          Pontefract

Crew of Halifax JP190

Sgt B.A. Bell   01/04/1944
                          Leeds (Lawns Wood) Cemetery

F/O J. Birkett   01/04/1944
                          Cremated Manchester Crematorium

F/Sgt P. Burchell   01/04/1944
                          Battersea (Modern) Cemetery

Sgt C. Farthing   01/04/1944
                        Grimsby (Scartho Road) Cemetery

Sgt J.G. Hinder   01/04/1944
                        Reading (Henley Road) Cemetery

F/O R.E.P. Ross MBE M.M.   01/04/1944
                        Chester (Blacon) Cemetery

Sgt H.W. Simpson   01/04/1944
                        Burton – upon – Trent Cemetery

Sgt H. Smith   01/04/1944
                        Oldham (Hollinwood) Cemetery

F/O J. Lees   19/09/1944 Halifax MZ908
                        Stonefall Cemetery, Harrogate

Crew of Halifax DK116

P/O H.G Haddrell   15/10/1944
                        Derry Hill (Christ Church)Churchyard

W.O. M.F. James   15/10/1944
                    Royston Church Additional Burial Ground

Sgt J.Nielson   15/10/1944
           Rugby (Clifton Road) Cemetery
W.O. G. Symonds   15/10/1944
           Rotheram (Moorgate) Cemetary
Sgt Moreaux   03/02/1943
Was once buried at East Chevington – Possibly repatriated to France

German

Crew of Ju 88
Lt. F. Gortain   28/05/1941
           Cannock Chase, Staffs. (Initially buried at Jedburgh)
Gfr. H. Matthius   28/05/1941
           Cannock Chase, Staffs. (Initially buried at Jedburgh)

Crew of Do217
Hauptman R. Frase   25/03/1943
           Dalston Road Cemetery, Carlisle
Gfr. S.Hartz   25/03/1943
           Not Known
Unteroffizier A. Ille   25/03/1943
           Dalston Road Cemetery, Carlisle
Unteroffizier W. Schneider   25/03/1943
           Dalston Road Cemetery, Carlisle

Crew of Ju 88
Unteroffizier K. Brinkmann   25/03/1943
       Cannock Chase, Staffs. (Initially buried Fogo Churchyard)
Unteroffizier E. Gluck   25/03/1943
       Cannock Chase, Staffs. (Initially buried Fogo Churchyard)
Hauptmann P. Rogge   25/03/1943
       Cannock Chase, Staffs. (Initially buried Fogo Churchyard)
Unteroffizier W. Walter   25/03/1943
           Not known

Sources

PRO Kew

AIR 16/167	Reports on casualties of enemy aircraft
AIR 16/960	Combat reports –Fighter Command
AIR 22/267	Places of crashes of enemy aircraft
AIR 22/278	Imports of aircraft from USA
AIR 25/51	ORB 3 Group, Bomber Command
AIR 25/60	Appendices to ORB 3 Group, Bomber Command
AIR 25/177, 178	ORB 9 Group & Appendices
AIR 27/48	ORB 4 Squadron
AIR 27/125	ORB 9 Squadron
AIR 27/141,147	ORB 10 Squadron and Appendices
AIR27/442	ORB 43 Squadron
AIR 27/731	ORB 90 Squadron
AIR 27/788	ORB 99 Squadron
AIR 27/1366	ORB 220 Squadron
AIR 27/1471	ORB 242 Squadron
AIR 27/1487	ORB 247 Squadron
AIR 27/1680	ORB 310 Squadron
AIR 27/1841	ORB 426 Squadron
AIR 27/1865	ORB 434 Squadron
AIR 28/17	ORB RAF Acklington
AIR 28/164	ORB RAF Clifton
AIR 28/248	ORB RAF East Moor
AIR 28/450	ORB RAF Leeming
AIR 28/479	ORB RAF Lindhome and 1656 HCU
AIR 28/680	ORB RAF Sandtoft and 1667 HCU
AIR 28/953	ORB RAF Wombleton
AIR 29/614	ORB 1666 HCU (previously 1679 Conv. Flt)
AIR 29/619	ORB 15EFTS
AIR 29/661	ORB 15 OTU
AIR 29/683	ORB 57 OTU
AIR 29/684	ORB 59 OTU
AIR 29/1002	ORB44MU
AIR 40/166	Intelligence reports on shot down German aircraft
AIR 40/2402-2412	Intelligence reports on shoot down German aircraft and their crews
AVIA 27/9	Reports on funerals, and graves for all ATA Personnel
AVIA 27/12	ATA Records

124

ADM 199/713,1267,1490,2007,2059   All relate to convoy SC94

Northumberland County Record Office, Morpeth

NC 9/3   Police Occurrence Book for Wooler

Sottish Borders Archive and Local History Centre, Selkirk

D/90/19/2   Register of Sudden Deaths, Roxburghshire 1941-43
D/90/19/3   Register of Sudden Deaths, Roxburghshire 1943-46

RAF Museum, Hendon

Form 78 and Form 1180 for each aircraft where available

Commonwealth War Graves Commission

Personal correspondence

Air Historical Branch, Ministry of Defence

Personal correspondence

Volksbund Deutsche Kriegsgraberfürsorge e.v.

Personal correspondence

Notes on Sources

  ORBs are a good source of information although they do tend to vary immensely in respect of both quantity and quality of the information from unit to unit. Every ORB includes Air Ministry Form 540 which is a daily diary of events but only operational squadrons ORBs include Form 541 which is an appendix listing individual flights of aircraft and their crews on operational missions. This inevitably leads to a discrepancy between the details available for the history of training unit aircraft and those available for operational unit aircraft.

  The tracing of airmen's service histories with any accuracy is almost impossible. Their records do exist but because of a Ministry of Defence ruling they can only be released to the airman himself or to his next of kin until 75 years from the date of death. The next of kin can give permission for such records to be released, but of course, without the records the next of kin are almost impossible to trace. An insoluble impasse. Occasionally, records can be traced backwards from one unit to another, but this method relies heavily on luck.

It is possible for official archives to contain mistakes. These mistakes can usually be identified by cross reference to other archive material but inevitably, in some cases, some doubt about recorded facts will still exist.

Bibliography

Bingham V.   Halifax – Second to None   Airlife 1986

Coupland P.   Straight and True – a History of RAF Leeming
                                                        Leo Cooper 1997

Delve K.   The Source Book of the RAF   Airlife 1994

Earl D.W.   Hell on High Ground   Airlife 1995

Fowler S., Elliot P., Nesbit R.C., and Goulter C.
                RAF Records in the PRO   PRO Publications 1994

Gorbett M. and Golding B.   Lancaster at War Vols 1,2, and 3
                                            Ian Allan 1971, 1979,1984

Freeman R.A.   The B – 17 Flying Fortress Story
                                            Arms and Armour 1998

Green W.   Famous Bombers of the Second World War
                                            Macdonald and James, 1975

Green W.   Famous Fighters of the Second World War
                                            Macdonald and James, 1975

Griehl M   Junkers Ju88   Arms and Armour 1990

Halpenny B.B.   Action Stations Vol 2
                                    Patrick Stephens 1981

Jefford C.G.   RAF Squadrons   Airlife 1988

Lumsden A.   British Aero Piston Engines and their Aircraft
                                    Airlife 1994

Milligan C.   Just a Few Lines – Riccarton Junction
                                    Copshaw Resource Centre

Rapier B.J.   Halifax at War   Ian Allan 1987

Smith D.J.   Action Stations Vol 7   Patrick Stephens 1983

            High Ground Wrecks
                    Midland Counties Publications 1989

Turner J.F.   V.Cs of the Air   Airlife 1993

Glossary

AB	Air bomber
A/C	Aircraft
AFU	Advance Flying Unit
AG	Air Gunner
ASR	Air- Sea Rescue
ATA	Air Transport Auxiliary
BBMF	Battle of Britain Memorial Flight
Cpl	Corporal
CWGC	Commonwealth War Graves Commission
D/F	Direction Finding
Draft Ewe	Ewe to old to either survive another year and/or have another lamb on the hill and sorted from the rest of the flock.
(E)FTS	(Elementary) Flying Training School
FE	Flight Engineer
F/L	Flight Lieutenant
F/O (RAF, RAAF, RCAF, RNZAF)	Flying Officer
F/O (USAAC, USAAF)	Flight Officer

F/Sgt	Flight Sergeant
Gather or "gathering"	Process of finding all the sheep on a hill and bringing them to one place.
"Gee"	Navigational and blind-bombing aid based on radio beams.
G/C	Group Captain
Gefreiter	German rank equivalent to British private
Gef	Gefreiter
GP	General Purpose
HCU	Heavy Conversion Unit
H2S	Blind bombing radar aid.
IFF	Identification, Friend or Foe
KG(German)	Kampfgeschwader (war or battlegroup).
LAC	Leading Aircraftsman
LANTIRN	Low altitude and night time infra red navigation
LLOTA	Low level overland training area
Mk	Mark i.e. Version
MU	Maintenance Unit
(M)UG	(Mid) Upper Gunner
Nacelle	"Pod" on the wing of an aircraft on or in which an engine is mounted
Obersfeldwebel	German rank equivalent to British corporal
O/L	Oberleutnant
O/Gef	Obergefreiter
ORB	Operational Record Book
OTU	Operational Training Unit
Pitot head	Hollow tube mounted on an aircraft to collect air passing the aircraft and connected to an instrument which then assess the speed of the aircraft from this flow of air.
P/O	Pilot Officer
QFI	Qualified Flying Instructor
RAAF	Royal Australian Air Force
RAFVR	Royal Air Force Volunteer Reserve
Radial Engine	One where the cylinders are arranged around the crankcase in a circle
RCAF	Royal Canadian Air Force
RG	Rear Gunner
RNZAF	Royal New Zealand Air Force
S/L	Squadron Leader
Sgt(s)	Sergeant(s)
"Shed"	Process of sorting sheep

Stall	When a wing or other flying surface (e.g. fin) ceases to create enough lift or force to either keep the aircraft airborne or on a stable flight due to insufficient speed or being at the wrong angle so that the developed force is not applied in the correct direction.
TFR	Terrain Following Radar
Unteroffizier	German rank equivalent to British sergeant
U/O	Unteroffizier
V-12	Engine where cylinders are in line with two rows of six cylinders mounted in a V-shape on the crankcase
W/C	Wing Commander
WO1	Warrant Officer(1)
WO2	Warrant Officer(2)
WO(p)	Wireless Operator

Battle Orders

Darkened field, the quiet night,
Silent planes awaiting flight.

Watchful ground crews waiting there
Stamp their feet in cold night air.

Smoke-filled crew room, dimly lit,
Young men donning flying kit.
Each with thoughts, though little said
About the night that lies ahead.

Maps and chutes and flying boots,
Helmets, masks and Irvin suits,
Flying rations, coffee flask,
Ready for the nightly task.

Transports waiting, climb aboard,
No more time can they afford
To worry over things not done.
Another trip, the time has come.

One by one the crews alight
To board their aircraft for the flight,
With nervous chatter, feeble joke;
A cigarette – the final smoke?

Takeoff time is almost here.
Tight smiles hide the gnawing fear
That, come the dawn, they may be found
As scattered fragments on the ground.

Engines started, props set fine,
Taxi out and wait in line.
Green light shining, it's your turn;
Now the insides start to churn.

Throttles open, engines roar.
Sweaty palms, the pulse rates soar.
Down the runway taking flight
Up into the black of night.
Sleepy Earth glides slowly by,
Whilst around in velvet sky
Friends are with you, through unseen,
Minds alert, the senses keen.

Now the friendly cliffs recede,
Soon to disappear and leave
Minds to ponder hours to come
And pray to see the morning Sun.

G.F. Dove

About The Author

Peter Clark was born in Melton Mowbray, Leicestershire, in 1943. Educated at King Edward VII County Grammar School, he went on to read Agricultural Biochemistry and Agriculture at the University of Wales, Aberystwyth, gaining an Honours Degree in Agriculture in 1967.

He worked as an Agricultural Officer in Tanzania, East Africa for two years before returning to the UK in 1970. After a brief spell in the Peak District, he came to Northumberland to manage the Roddam Estate in 1971.

He has had an interest in military aircraft, both old and new, since boyhood. This interest, together with the location of his home, nestled against the foothills of the Cheviots, provided the stimulus to produce "Where the Hills Meet the Sky". The interest which this book created encouraged him to investigate other crashes in the wider Border area, which has resulted in the production of this new guide.

He married his wife, Chris, whilst in Tanzania, and they have a son and daughter, both grown up.

Index

Thompson, F/O R (RCAF) 82
Thornton, Sgt E 57
Thornton, James 41
Turner, P/O J 105
Turnhouse 48,65
Tweedale, Sgt 52

V

Valley 5,37,67-68,95

W

Walter, V/O W 74,123
Warr, F/O B (RCAF) 82
Williams, Sgt 52
Winfield 9,91
Winstanley, P/O T 72,121
Womack, P/O W.T.A 39
Wombleton 78,124
Wood, Sgt J.W 57
Wood, Sgt (Police) 80
Wright, Sgt 30,56

Z

Zacharias, Holge 109